MOMENTS THAT...
THAT...
COULD'VE
CHANGED
FOOTBALL
FOREVER
WHAT IF..?

PETER PRICKET &
PETER THORNTON

MOMENTS THAT... COULD'VE CHANGED FOOTBALL FOREVER WHAT IF..?

First published by Pitch Publishing, 2023

Pitch Publishing
9 Donnington Park,
85 Birdham Road,
Chichester,
West Sussex,
PO20 7AJ
www.pitchpublishing.co.uk
info@pitchpublishing.co.uk

A CIP catalogue record is available for this book
from the British Library.

ISBN 978 1 80150 451 5

Typesetting and origination by Pitch Publishing

Printed and bound in Great Britain by TJ Books, Padstow

CONTENTS

PETER PRICKETT
INTRODUCTION

I once heard Jürgen Klopp described as 'an expert with the soul of a child'. I have no idea who said it, or if those are the precise words, but the idea of it stuck with me. Our expertise should not make us boring or numb. Our expertise should heighten our awareness, increase the wonder and excitement with which we view events. That expertise should widen the potential for joyous possibilities and flights of the imagination.

As a child I fantasised about football. What if such and such a player had signed for my team? What if we hadn't hit the post? What if the team won all of the remaining games of the season? Why couldn't this happen? All things are possible to a child.

Football allows those who follow it to retain much of their childish joy but as they get older experience erodes the fantasy. Cynicism creeps in and supporters want to see the evidence first before investing time in imagining that could be better spent streaming movies or tweeting their fury.

While watching one such movie my mind started to wander. An ordinary day of social media saw the usual barrage of Messi versus Ronaldo rows to 'finally decide who is the greatest of all time'. My thinking was 'who cares?' Both are clearly extraordinary players who football fans of the era have been fortunate enough to be able to enjoy simultaneously. Stop wasting time and energy fighting over them, when there are far more interesting ways to enjoy them. Such as imagining the two of them playing together. (It's Messi by the way, the answer is Messi, sorry Ronaldo fans.) It struck me that the concept could potentially be a good series of blogs. I started with imagining the two most dominant players of the modern game playing together. Through social media I asked if anyone else would like to contribute, thus creating a three-pronged take on how it might work if Messi and Ronaldo were team-mates. I must thank Jim Kearns and Hiko Seijuro for their contributions to that first post. Though there is a Messi and Ronaldo chapter in this book it is quite different to the original, which can be found online.

Peter Thornton read the post and immediately called me. 'We have to write this book.' Peter and I had discussed football and various projects with each other for years but never worked together. He was adamant that I should forget the blog idea, this was a book. Having already written three books at that stage I didn't need a lot of encouraging. What I did need to do was drop the other books I had been toying with and get focused.

In a Manchester hotel the idea was given further shape. What should we include? Which players? Which teams? Incidents and stories have a tendency to attach to certain sides and if we were not careful this could have become a book filled with solely tales related to Manchester United, Liverpool and England. We wanted to avoid that as much as possible, which means that some seemingly obvious ideas have been left out. If the answer to the hypothetical question is no more interesting than 'they would have won the league' then it was not deemed rich enough or impactful enough to feature. Especially if the team in question already had several titles to their name.

While experimenting with subject ideas I took to Twitter and ran a poll asking, 'Who would win, Brazil 1970 or Spain 2008–12?' The fury of the responses was taken as further evidence that we needed to write this book.

All subjects were subject to two parts. Part one was extensive research to outline the events as they were. Part two was a flight of fancy. The writer taking the concept and running with it as they saw fit. I could return to the child in my soul and imagine the wonder of an alternative timeline. The greatness or drama that we missed out in reality playing out first in my mind, then on the page. I don't mind telling you that real fun was had writing these takes but also a great number were deleted. Choosing which European club Pelé might have played for threw out some great discussions and pairing him with Eusébio was incredibly tempting, but that had to go in favour of something a little more realistic. Even fantasy requires some suspension of disbelief.

This leads me to one final place. If I ended up disagreeing with my own ideas then it is highly likely that the reader will disagree too! We want you to! If you have disagreed then it means our writing has achieved its goal. It has got you thinking. You have gone on your own flight of fantasy, returning to childhood wonder. Prompted by our assertions to make your own and played out the events of history in a different way. Now you have your own little alternative reality to occupy. Used your imagination to create something wonderful.

I hope you enjoy that as much as you enjoy our book.

PETER THORNTON
INTRODUCTION

We met through our love of coaching on social media. Several long conversations over the phone later, and we found we shared similar views about the game itself and how it should be played. Although we both have teams that we support, we both have a lifelong love of the game of football. We are able to take off our blue and red tinted spectacles and look at what happens objectively. (Most of the time!)

As much as it is the skills of the game and the controversial moments that get fans talking, it is often the 'what ifs' that spark the really animated conversations and the dividing lines in opinion. These are what bind football fans together, not just the endless possibilities that DID happen during 90 minutes, never mind a season, but the almost limitless number of variations that COULD HAVE happened. We'd both had ideas about those 'what if' moments in football. During one of our lengthy chats those thoughts crystallised into what has become this book.

One afternoon we made a list of all of our favourite 'moments' that could have changed football for ever. Our criteria for narrowing the list down was how much of a knock-on effect a particular 'moment' had going forward, on a player, a manager, a club or even the game of football itself. We didn't really go for 'if Roy Race doesn't miss that open goal Melchester Rovers would have won the cup' moments because they are pretty one-dimensional. We tended to go for moments that, when projected further, had real knock-on effects that would have changed the course of football history. Then, because we are both heavily into the coaching side of the game, we looked at what we call 'fantasy match-ups'. So what if one great team from one era had played a great team from another? We wanted to try and combat the recency bias of the modern-day football supporter, to try to illustrate different coaching philosophies and predict the outcomes.

These are our 'what if' moments. We have quite a few others. Some will disagree with our list. Some will believe there would have been different outcomes to the ones we arrived at. Some will want to take what we have outlined even further. Ultimately that is what we want. To set football fans talking about the game. To give their ideas an airing. If they like our take on things, then brilliant. If they have completely the opposite opinions then let's hear them. Because 'what if' everyone agrees with us, isn't as much fun.

WHAT IF ERIC CANTONA
HADN'T RETIRED?

King Eric. The catalyst for Manchester United's reign of dominance. Signed from Leeds for just over £1 million in 1992, he was the final piece in Sir Alex Ferguson's Manchester United puzzle. After rumoured attempts to sign David Hirst, Matthew Le Tissier, Brian Deane and Alan Shearer, Manchester United signed Dion Dublin, but a broken leg early in the 1992/93 season stopped Dublin's career at Old Trafford before it could even start. United were once again on the lookout for a striker. In November of 1992, they landed Eric Cantona.

Cantona's impact went beyond goalscoring. Describing Cantona as a striker is to suggest his role was as the primary goalscorer. While he scored regularly his creativity elevated Manchester United to the next level. Cantona brought with him flair, swagger and attitude. His confidence filled the team, the training ground and Old Trafford itself. With Eric around nothing was impossible. Cantona propelled Manchester United to the Premier League trophy in 1992/93, following this up with wins in 93/94, 95/96 and 96/97. Two FA Cup wins would also arrive, in 93/94 and 95/96. Cantona scored three goals in the two finals, including a famous step-back volley winner against fierce rivals Liverpool in 1996. This was just one of many iconic moments provided by the man with the upturned collar. From a perfectly spun outside of the foot assist to Denis Irwin, a thunderous free kick beyond the grasp of David Seaman (with an exuberant, plaster cast-wielding celebration) to the impudent, exquisite chip versus Sunderland at Old Trafford. As well as iconic moments he had a penchant for vital goals, match-winning goals. During the first of Manchester United's title wins Cantona seemed to specialise in scoring the only goal in a 1-0 win. In 1995/96 Manchester United came back from 12 points behind to overtake Newcastle United. In the crucial away game at St James' Park Cantona scored the only goal.

Cantona retired from football at the end of the 1996/97 season. He was 30 years old when he played his final game for Manchester United and showing little indication that his powers were on the wane. He was an icon, perhaps *the* modern-day icon, and a legend in his own playing career. For many players it is only once they have retired that their place in history is assured, but for Cantona that position was abundantly clear. The player who was instrumental in winning United's first league title for 26 years, then delivering three more. Inspiring and guiding a generation of young players who would become known as the class of '92. At times as much credit seemed to be given to Cantona as to Sir Alex Ferguson.

How long could Cantona have continued? Even if he had retired at 33 (still relatively early) he would certainly have been playing in 2000. Had he retired at 35 that would have taken him to 2002. This covers the famous treble of Premier League, Champions League and FA Cup in 1998/99, and two more Premier League wins in 1999/2000 and 2000/01. Cantona might have added more titles to his already legendary haul.

Or would he?

The replacement for Cantona was Teddy Sheringham. The Tottenham Hotspur and England striker was a vastly experienced player with the ability to both score and create. His playing style seemed to be a perfect like-for-like replacement for King Eric.

It didn't quite work out that way.

Sheringham's personality was not as large as Cantona's. Although the class remained, the swagger and confidence had dropped away. Infamously, Sheringham's relationship with his strike partner Andy (Andrew) Cole was also frosty. Once Cole arrived Cantona went from the player United looked to for goals, to a creator and scorer of important goals. Cole scored 15 league goals during Sheringham's first season, while Teddy himself netted nine times, a relatively low combined total. Manchester United finished the 1997/98 season without a trophy, Sheringham judged to have been a flop.

Manchester United were never a club to wait on a problem to resolve itself, especially when it came to the vital business of scoring goals. Dwight Yorke had been a consistent scorer for Aston Villa. Manchester United moved for him, spending just over £12.5 million, a huge fee for the time. The Cole and Yorke partnership became legendary, with the pair of them combining for 35 league goals in the 1998/99 league season. They followed this with 39 goals in the 99/00 season. Sheringham was reduced to a rotational role, which he shared with Ole Gunnar Solskjaer.

It was this quartet of forwards that became famous for firing Manchester United to their legendary treble. Solskjaer weighed in with a dozen league goals plus a further half dozen in other competitions. Sheringham only contributed five in all competitions, one in the FA Cup Final, another of vital importance.

On 26 May 1999 Bayern Munich have dominated Manchester United for 90 minutes. Bayern have rattled the frame of the goal twice but only lead 1-0. United haven't looked like winning the game but they have a corner.

Most football followers know exactly what comes next. A Beckham corner is half-cleared, Ryan Giggs scuffs a right-footed shot into the penalty area, the ball reaches Sheringham who pivots on his standing leg, sweeping the ball into the net with his right foot to equalise.

Minutes later another Beckham corner from the left side is headed towards goal by Sheringham. Solskjaer is lurking at the far post. He reacts to poke a volley into the roof of the Bayern net. United have gone from beaten to winners in mere minutes and it is the substitutes who break Bayern hearts.

When Cantona retired he was the first name on the team sheet and captain of the side. Had he remained until he was 33 or 35 years old, in all likelihood Teddy Sheringham would not have been signed; United would not have had any need for him. As Sheringham was not the success United had hoped for, they signed Yorke. The retirement of Cantona was the catalyst for the formation of the front four who clinched the treble but if Cantona had not retired when he did, Sheringham would not have been in the team to contribute in the vital moments of the final. United might have performed differently on the day with Cantona in the team, who is to say? Then again, they may not have even made it to the final.

Cantona's retirement also left a vacancy as captain. Roy Keane filled the role magnificently. Keane's leadership played a huge role in United's post-Cantona dominance, with the game-by-game impact almost impossible to measure. However, in United's journey to Champions League triumph Keane left a highly measurable mark with one of the great captain's performances.

In the semi-final Manchester United faced a Juventus side laced with Zidane, Davids, Deschamps and co, managed by Carlo Ancelotti. At Old Trafford the game had finished 1-1, leaving United a tough task to get through to the final. The task became even tougher when

Filipo Inzaghi scored twice within 11 minutes. Keane powered in a header to drag United back into the game before picking up a yellow card that would mean he missed the final. This personal blow did not stop him from grabbing control of the game from central midfield and inspiring United to a 3-2 win in the Stadio Delle Alpi.

Does Roy Keane lead the team in this way without the armband? Leadership does not have to be about captaincy but Keane clearly relished the role. Cantona was a great inspiration, Keane was a great general.

If Cantona doesn't retire he certainly adds to his collection of trophies, but do United win a treble and the likes of Beckham, Scholes, Keane, Neville and Solskjaer command quite so significant a place in United history?

There is a strong case to be made that if Cantona does not retire Manchester United do not win the treble in 1998/99 and the course of football history is quite different.

WHAT IF THERE WAS NO OFFSIDE LAW?

A beautiful through ball splits a defence wide open. The centre-forward takes the ball in his stride, glides past the outstretched goalkeeper, and rolls the ball into the gaping net. The gasps of expectation as he breaks clear are eclipsed by a thunderclap of noise as he scores. Only for the roar to die on the lips of thousands as the linesman raises his flag to indicate the centre-forward was inches offside.

Every football fan for generations had been brought down to earth in the cruellest of fashions. Linesmen became the focal point of the fans' wrath. Bad enough when lost in the throng of a cacophonous crowd, but unnerving when voiced by half a dozen die-hards often standing less than six feet away at the lower levels of the game.

Then came VAR. Now the moment of despair is delayed. Now the linesman's flag has not gone up, but after the exultation of a goal being scored, as the teams are walking back to the centre circle to kick off, the referee hears a voice in his earpiece. The crowd groans. There is a delay that seems like an eternity. The action is replayed in a studio far away frame by frame. Lines are drawn on screen. We are not talking inches offside now. We are talking a hair's breadth. The goal is disallowed. Now it is the fans of the team that had conceded who celebrate.

For many fans, offside is seen as a blight on the game of football. It prevents the joy of a goal being scored. It denies them their moments of glory. It frustrates managers and players alike. So, what if there was no offside in football? What would the game look like then? Would it produce more high-scoring matches that would entertain us more?

The concept of 'offside' has been around since the hybrid 'football' games that were played in public schools in the mid-1800s. It was felt 'bad form' to have players 'ahead of the ball'. Those early football games were very much about one man with the ball 'charging' at the other side. The Cambridge Rules of 1863 state: '**When a player has kicked the ball anyone of the same side who is nearer the opponent's goal line is out of play.**' The first revision came in 1866 and now there had to be '... **at least three of his opponents between him and their own goal ...**'

Before this change 'dribbling' was still the main form of attack, with other forwards ready to take over if the man with the ball lost control or was tackled. Now the passing game was able to develop. The choice of 'at least three' defenders was based on the embryonic formations that usually saw a goalkeeper and two full-backs behind eight forwards. As the passing game grew, players dropped between the forwards and the full-backs to become 'half-backs'. The 2-3-5 formation was born. Of course, the full-backs of the 1870s did not play like the full-backs of today and would be more recognisable as centre-halves in the modern game.

The FA were always looking to try to make football more attractive to the masses that thronged to watch it. Offside seems to have been a regular focal point of debate even in the early days. In 1907 the law was changed so no player could be offside in his own half. It is difficult to imagine how that worked but play was often confined to a narrow strip, as even the deepest defenders pushed forward. This basic tactic added neither goals nor excitement to the game. Fourteen years later, to try to give further advantage to attacking play, there would be no offside from a throw-in, a law exploited to the full by Rory Delap 80 years later.

By the mid-1920s teams had started to perfect the 'offside trap'. Newcastle United had six 0-0 draws in succession. Goals were on the decline across all of football. Crowds were dropping. It prompted the FA to take a further look at offside. The result was that the law was changed so there only needed to be two defenders, including the goalkeeper, between the attacking team and the goal line. This immediately made the offside trap a far riskier defensive option. Goals were on the increase again.

There have been some minor tweaks to the law since then but the two defenders principle has remained constant. We have seen 'level with the last defender', 'body parts' like arms and legs excluded, and a new interpretation on 'interfering with play' introduced in the last 30 years. But we stand with what Bill Shankly said: 'If a player is not interfering with play, or seeking to gain an advantage, then he should be.'

It is interesting to look at the shape of other invasive games that are played with a ball that do not have offside. Both Aussie Rules and Gaelic football allow players in all parts of the pitch at all times. What is first noticeable is that both games are played on a field much bigger than that of football. Both games are played with more players too, 18 in Aussie Rules and 15 in Gaelic football, but there is definitely more space available on the pitch. Both games involve running with the ball in the hand. In Gaelic football it must be bounced every five steps and in Aussie Rules every 16 yards. The object of both games is to score points through kicking the ball into a goal or between the posts. There is much overlap in the two codes. Watching either game for the first time it is impossible to miss how many long-punted kicks there are, either to move the ball upfield, or as an attempt on the goal itself. Catching the ball is a key skill in both games. There appears to be less cohesive team play and more individual battles than in association football.

Played with an oval ball, Aussie Rules leans more towards rugby football. Played with a round ball, Gaelic leans more towards association football. This is evident in the size of the players. The laws and rules of any game have a direct effect on the size of the people who play it. Rugby league once had large forwards and smaller backs. Once uncontested scrums were introduced, the size of the players has become almost uniform, while in rugby union, with the lineout still prominent, there are giants playing alongside players who would just be considered 'big' in other sports. The beauty of football in its present form is that players of all different sizes and shapes can play it. Perhaps the goalkeeper is the only position where size does matter, with very few top-class keepers below six feet tall and most a good few inches taller.

So what would association football look like if there was no offside?

Players are now allowed in any area of the pitch at any time. We would surely see teams leave attacking players upfield and to combat this there would surely be defensive players left behind to mark them. With these attacking players upfield there is no incentive to create build-up play, to try to move defenders. The modern goalkeeper can already kick the ball the full length of the field. Now their skill would come in being able to target a team-mate in the opposition penalty box. This accuracy in long punting would become a must for any defender too. The attacking team can now add other players upfield in the hope for 'second ball' knock-downs from the long punt.

Play is concentrated in and around the penalty area. Wide players are used to deliver crosses when a long punt is recycled by the attacking team. With team-mates able to stand anywhere, there is less emphasis on dribbling to beat a man and more emphasis on returning the ball back into the penalty area. The long punt is now aimed into an area as opposed to a specific player, as three or more attackers can run from both behind and in front of defenders. If a defending team won the ball back from a long punt, would any coach be brave enough to 'play out' and leave the opposition forwards behind them, knowing that if they lost possession again, these attackers would have a free run on goal?

Whenever possession is lost the team now with the ball can counter-attack immediately with the long punt forward. Is there any value to playing through midfield? Possession lost in the centre circle would mean a shorter, more accurate punt forward. Would possession in midfield entice the defenders forward to try to win the ball? Again, they could immediately pay a high price with unmarked attackers in the penalty area. With no offside law, the midfield would be likely to become redundant. Both penalty areas would become congested. There is no point in the defending team playing a defensive line like a back four. Coordination in the defensive unit no longer works. Defending becomes very much man-marking. Attackers now use their speed and trickery to lose their man as the long punt comes in. Being able to head the ball accurately to a team-mate or at goal becomes ever more important.

With no offside a key defensive component, as ever, is the goalkeeper. But now not so much as a shot-stopper. Now they have to be able to jump and catch those long punts into the penalty area. With the current offside law, a modern goalkeeper touches the ball eight times as often with their feet as with their hands. With no offside this figure would surely tilt back towards more touches with their hands, as their 'possession' is reduced to the long punt upfield.

Football would become a game played by giants. Height becomes a key factor in winning the ball, and weight in retaining it. Footballers would resemble the lineout players in rugby union. The days of a Messi, of a Maradona, would be over. There would be no midfield geniuses because there would be no midfield. The basic formation would become 5-0-5. Somewhere there is a tactical genius, a Guardiola or a Klopp, who finds a different way.

Defenders will always look to relieve pressure. One option would be to have a defender waiting slightly in front of the other four to take the ball from a knock-down, or from a team-mate. With an ocean of space in front, there would be the opportunity to break forward beyond the five opposing attackers. At the other end of the pitch, one of his five team-mates could drop out from the attacking five to receive the ball. Is this how the

5-0-5 evolves to a 4-1-1-4? Is this how football reclaims its midfield?

What if a team pulled all ten outfield players back into their own penalty area from the goal kick restart? The coach is trying to combat the goalkeeper targeting his centre-forwards and negating any knock-downs. Do defenders go up? Or do they still stay back? If the ten-man defence wins the ball, do they counter in the traditional manner? What appears to be a totally defensive option, now looks like it can create space for an attacking team to break into. What would happen if the defensive team pushed up to halfway? If the attacking team lost possession breaking out there are lots of gaps for the team which regains the ball to exploit.

If there is no offside, does the attacking team mark the goalkeeper? If an attacker can stand anywhere on the pitch, so long as there is no physical obstruction involved, the goalkeeper becomes a player who can be marked. The law regarding how long a keeper can hold the ball would have to be enforced rigidly to prevent a stand-off when a keeper has the ball in their hands.

With long punts into the penalty area now standard, there is unlikely to be a drop in goalscoring opportunities. These would come off direct headers, second ball knock-downs, and being able to receive the ball and shoot from any part of the field. So the original premise, that the removal of offside would create more excitement, more goalscoring opportunities and more goals, is up for debate.

What the current offside law does, is to give football its fluidity. The depth of the defensive line dictates the space available on the field. The way the lines of defence, midfield and attack move out of possession dictates the ebb and flow of the game. Attackers have a constant problem to solve. How to get through or around these defensive lines. The skills that have developed to do this are what makes football the beautiful game. The movement and the game intelligence of attacking players, the tricks they can do with the football, the risks they take, are what capture the imagination of fans the world over. Without offside we have a different contest altogether, where the long punt is king and no one under 6ft 3in is getting a game.

Without offside and with all the other current laws in place, football simply does not resemble the game loved by millions. One development from this is that we would very likely see a referee in each half, probably in each penalty area, to scrutinise the numerous challenges for the high ball. But what if we take away offside and apply one simple new law – no heading? What would football look like then? With the evidence growing on the damage heading can cause to the brain, how the game would look without one of football's basic skills may be here sooner than we think.

WHAT IF CELTIC AND RANGERS HAD JOINED THE PREMIER LEAGUE?

In 1992 English football experienced a watershed moment. The Premier League emerged. At first many thought it would merely be a rebranding but over time the changes were much more powerful and fundamental, changing the Premier League into the powerhouse that we see today.

In the decades since, English football has been at the heights of the European and global game. Increased status and revenues have seen imports of exceptional quality push the standards ever higher. At one time imports into English football came from Northern Ireland, the Republic of Ireland, Scotland and Wales; now imports come from all corners of the planet, with the home nations left trailing behind. This was not always the case, as Scottish football was once genuinely as strong as the English game, with periods where it was arguably stronger. Celtic were the first British team to win the European Cup and in the 1980s and 90s Scottish teams were competing for major European honours.

Leeds United were the last champions before the Premier League era. Rangers the champions of Scotland. The two faced each other in the second round of the inaugural Champions League. Rangers went through, beating Leeds 2-1 home and away. Leeds scored first in the first game at Ibrox through a stunning Gary McAllister volley, thumped into the top corner from outside the penalty area. That was as good as it got for Leeds. Shortly after, their goalkeeper John Lukic left his line to punch away a corner, but the ball slid off the back of his gloves and into his own net. The embarrassment was not just felt by Lukic, but the whole of England. Ally McCoist poached a second goal from inside the six-yard box to seal the first leg.

At Elland Road Mark Hateley smashed a 20-yard volley past Lukic before supplying a cross for his strike partner McCoist to head home. Leeds pulled back a late goal but it was all too late. Scotland had triumphed in the Battle of Britain.

In the first Champions League season Rangers had a tremendous European campaign. The format was such that after a number of knockout ties teams reached a group stage. Rangers were in the same group as Marseille, Club Brugge and CSKA Moscow. Arguably they had the easier draw with Milan, IFK Gothenburg, Porto and PSV Eindhoven in the other group. Milan crushed everyone in their group, winning six games out of six to reach the final. Rangers' group was much tighter. The Glasgow club would not lose a game, but won two and drew four. At this time the format was two points for a win, making the draws incredibly valuable. Marseille won three and drew three, edging into the final by a single point. The world expected Milan to triumph but Marseille won the final 1-0.

The subplot is that Marseille were subsequently found guilty of match-fixing at this time. Both Milan and Rangers have reason to feel aggrieved by this dark mark on the history of the Champions League.

Rangers had a very strong team in 1992. Graeme Souness had been able to attract players from England and Serie A. When he departed for Liverpool his successor, Walter Smith, inherited a strong group that would grow stronger in the following seasons. In 1992/93 the England players Hateley and Trevor Steven featured regularly alongside Scotland internationals McCoist, Richard Gough, Andy Goram and Ian Durrant. Hateley joined Rangers from Monaco and Steven signed from Everton not long after they had won the second of their league titles in the middle of the 1980s. Rangers had also signed Alexei Mykhaylychenko from Serie A champions Sampdoria. Rangers were able to attract players from an impressive array of clubs. In 1994 Brian Laudrup signed from Fiorentina and Basile Boli from Marseille. A year later Oleg Salenko, winner of the Golden Boot at the 1994 World Cup, signed from Valencia. More significantly, Paul Gascoigne joined from Lazio.

Rangers were utterly dominant in Scotland at this time, winning nine straight league titles as well as making significant inroads into European competition. Celtic were forced to respond. When they halted the Rangers run their recruitment had brought in manager Wim Jansen and signed Henrik Larsson from Feyenoord and Paul Lambert from Borussia Dortmund. Two seasons earlier Dortmund had been European champions. In the 2020s it is hard to imagine Celtic signing a key player from a top Bundesliga team.

Rangers' success in the Champions League was in contrast to the early performances of English clubs. Leeds were seen off by Rangers themselves and the next season Manchester United represented England in the Champions League, as they would for the next two seasons. This was the time of their Galatasaray nightmares. In 1993/94 they seemed to be in complete control against Galatasaray before scrambling to a 3-3 draw at home. A 0-0 away from home saw them ousted on away goals.

The next season United faced Galatasaray in the group, drawing 0-0 before beating them 4-0 at home. Unfortunately it was too late as defeats in Gothenburg and Barcelona meant it was impossible for them to qualify. They finished third in the group. It would not be until the 1996/97 edition of the Champions League that an English club got beyond the group stage of the competition, with Manchester United losing out in the semi-final against Dortmund.

If performance in Europe is an indicator of the relative strength of the best teams in a domestic league, Rangers were certainly a match for Manchester United.

A popular source of debate has been how Rangers and Celtic would perform in England. The restart in 1992 would have provided an excellent window for them to join. Manchester United were the first champions, with Aston Villa second and Norwich City third. There can be little doubt that Rangers were a superior team to Villa and Norwich.

While they may not have been able to finish as champions they could easily have secured second place. The heavyweights of English football were struggling, with Liverpool and Arsenal some way off the pace. Manchester City and Chelsea were not a factor, their takeovers many years away. It is not too fanciful to imagine that Celtic could squeeze into a top six of Manchester United, Aston Villa, Norwich City, newly promoted Blackburn Rovers, QPR and Liverpool.

The financial windfall and raise in profile from a combination of Champions League and Premier League performances would have allowed Rangers to recruit aggressively. Manchester United were superb in the 1993/94 season but in 94/95 big-spending Blackburn Rovers edged Manchester United out and finished as champions. Rangers, with their strengthening squad and strong manager, would have been quite capable of a similar feat.

During this period the Premier League television deal was significant but the bigger financial factors were Champions League money and attendances. For Manchester United the increasing size of Old Trafford kick-started their financial progress. Both Rangers and Celtic would have been very well placed in this regard with two of the largest football stadiums in Britain. Their potential for revenues in the early 1990s was much stronger than the likes of Arsenal, Chelsea and Manchester City.

With this early foothold the Glasgow clubs could have pushed their way to the top of the Premier League and stayed there for some time. Rangers may never have financially collapsed and the great lull in Scottish football may have been avoided. Indeed, the idea of 'Scottish football' versus 'English football' may have eroded completely. This was always the fear and largely the reason that the Scottish giants have never joined, but there is little doubt they would be competitive and that joining would have been better for Rangers, Celtic and the Premier League itself.

WHAT IF RONALDO AND MESSI HAD PLAYED TOGETHER?

For ten years in a row the men's Ballon d'Or was won by either Lionel Messi or Cristiano Ronaldo. Messi won the 2021 award to take his personal tally to seven. Ronaldo has five wins. To put these numbers into context the next most wins belong to Johan Cruyff, Michel Platini and Marco van Basten, all with three wins.

Who is the best? This question will likely be asked forever. People were not allowed to value them equally. The question demanded an answer. An answer that revealed how one viewed football. The artistry and joy of Messi or the relentless hunger of Ronaldo? The growth hormone cheating of Messi or the selfish egotism of Ronaldo? Followers of football split down the middle.

They are considered to be great rivals, seemingly driving one another on to greater feats of scoring. This perception was at its peak during Ronaldo's time at Real Madrid, with Barcelona's Messi and Madrid's Ronaldo facing off in *El Clásico*, Spanish football's hottest match-up. Messi and Ronaldo's presence elevated the contest to global status.

The Messi and Ronaldo rivalry first took shape when Messi's Barcelona clashed with Ronaldo's Manchester United in the 2009 Champions League Final in Rome. Messi scored as Barcelona won 2-0. That summer Real Madrid paid a then world record fee of £80 million to bring Ronaldo to the Santiago Bernabeu.

For nine dramatic and thrilling years Ronaldo and Messi would grace La Liga at the same time, their two clubs dominating in both Spain and Europe. During this period Ronaldo and Real won two league titles and four Champions Leagues. Messi and Barcelona won six league titles and two Champions Leagues.

Messi played in two superteams: the Pep Guardiola side famed for tiki-taka built around the axis of Xavi and Iniesta, then the three seasons of Messi, Suárez and Neymar. The three superstar forwards linked up for three seasons for over 360 goals combined.

Ronaldo played in the second Galactico era, headed up by himself, with José Mourinho as the Galactico manager. This team, including Kaka, Ozil, Alonso, Higuain, Kroos and more, eventually won a single league title. Ronaldo would not win a Champions League until Carlo Ancelotti arrived. The next Madrid superteam saw Zinedine Zidane become manager, winning three straight Champions League tournaments.

All the while Ronaldo and Messi pounded in the goals. Messi had a remarkable 91-goal calendar year in 2012. In the 2011/12 season Messi scored 50 league goals. In the same season Ronaldo scored 46 league goals. Ronaldo's best league season total was 48 in 2014/15. Messi only managed 43 goals that campaign. Ronaldo would amass 450 goals for Real Madrid in 438 games. Messi scored 472 goals in 476 games during the same period.

No wonder their identities became intertwined as legendary opponents. Could the story have been different?

What if the two had joined forces?

Barcelona's reputation is as youth developers, promoting great individuals from within. It is Real Madrid who spend out the millions on Galacticos. In summer 2009 surely there is no way that Barcelona would pay £80 million to bring in Ronaldo? Realistically this is the only moment in which a recognisable Messi and Ronaldo could play together. It is possible Barcelona sign Ronaldo from Sporting Lisbon but the tricky winger was a very different player to the one who arrived at Real Madrid from Manchester United, an entertainer versus a proficient goalscorer. That summer Barcelona signed Zlatan Ibrahimovic from Inter. The deal was a part-exchange sending Samuel Eto'o to Inter, Barcelona paying a fee reported by some sources to be as high as £59 million.

Could Barcelona have persuaded Manchester United to accept a similar amount plus Eto'o for Ronaldo?

In our version of reality, United go for the deal, softening the blow of losing both Ronaldo and Tevez in the same summer.

Neither player was a centre-forward. Messi played wide on the right, drifting infield and with freedom to roam. Ronaldo had been prolific for Manchester United from the left-hand side, interchanging with the centre-forward (the United forward line of Ronaldo, Tevez and Rooney was remarkably fluid, with all three able to play wide or centrally). During Ronaldo's early seasons at Real Madrid he played wide, scoring 40 league goals as an inside-forward. Tactically Barcelona could have incorporated both players.

The Barcelona squad for the 2009/10 season would have also included Thierry Henry and Pedro, both of whom were capable of filling the centre-forward position. Henry rarely played a central role for Barcelona, though he spent the majority of his career with Arsenal and France as a central striker. The description of Henry as a central striker even in his time at Arsenal did not quite fit the bill. Henry was listed in line-ups alongside Bergkamp at numbers 9 and 10, but he did not play like a classic number 9, through the middle of the pitch, up against the opposition central defenders. Henry would often pull out into a wide left position, away from the central defenders and towards the full-backs. From here he would cut inside to combine or execute his famous right-footed curved finish.

This trait of Henry's could dovetail extremely well with Ronaldo's style of play at that time. Ronaldo would start wide on the left of a 4-3-3 system, either receiving the ball wide or drifting into the centre, occupying a centre-forward role. For many seasons Ronaldo dovetailed superbly with Karim Benzema, whose role was to move defenders out of position and create spaces for others, often pulling wide or deep from what would be considered a centre-forward position. Thierry Henry's intelligent movement and drifting into space from the centre-forward position would enable Ronaldo to get into his favoured goalscoring areas.

What of Messi?

Messi performed in a similar way for Barcelona, mainly operating on the right-hand side but floating into advanced positions to score or create. In this system, with Henry pulling to the left, Ronaldo and Messi could appear to be in the centre-forward positions. Messi's movement infield from the right side created ample opportunities for Dani Alves to overlap (or underlap) on the right. Centrally the magnificent trio of Busquets, Iniesta and Xavi would circulate the ball, leaving the Barcelona style relatively unaltered by the arrival of Ronaldo. Pep Guardiola's mesmerising tiki-taka would remain with one additional option – Ronaldo's ability to attack his full-back in the air produced vast numbers of goals at Real Madrid. On the right-hand side Barcelona would have Dani Alves, whose ability to provide exquisite crosses at Sevilla helped propel him into the spotlight. The potential connection between Alves' crosses and Ronaldo's headers provides an additional option to Barcelona's attacking play.

Tactically this could clearly work. The next issue is whether Ronaldo and Messi could co-exist? Over the years it has become a commonly held belief that both players have big egos (perhaps the general consensus being that Ronaldo's is the bigger). Messi seemingly seeing off star players to ensure that he remained the main man, while Ronaldo would often appear furious with team-mates if they had the temerity to score rather than feed him for an opportunity.

However, both players featured in their own fantastic attacking trios alongside superstar players. Messi linked up with Neymar and Suárez at Barcelona between 2014 and 2017. Neymar scored 39, 31 and 20 goals in those three seasons. Suárez scored 25, 59 and 37 goals. Messi scored 58, 41 and 54. These numbers show us that Messi could score in high volume even while his team-mates were also scoring large quantities of goals.

From 2013 until 2018 Ronaldo formed an attacking trio with Karim Benzema and Gareth Bale. The numbers for this trio were not quite as evenly spread and a couple of seasons were impacted by injuries to Bale. Nonetheless, their goal tallies read thus: Benzema scored 24, 22, 28, 19 and 12. Bale scored 22, 17, 19, 9 (injury-hit season) and 21. Ronaldo scored 51, 61, 51, 42 and 44. Quite clearly Ronaldo dominated his trio far more than Messi did, but the other players still scored very healthy numbers of goals.

In their first season together it is quite likely that Thierry Henry would have scored a lower tally of goals, sacrificing a little of his own game to unleash the capabilities of the two legendary players. The 2009/10 season was Henry's final season at Barcelona and his powers were on the downswing. Henry likely scores little better than double figures; Ronaldo scored 33 goals in his first season in Madrid. A combination of injuries and bedding in limited him to 35 games. It is not unreasonable to think that Ronaldo scores around 35 times for Barcelona. Messi scored 47 goals in 2009/10, so again it is quite reasonable to suggest Messi nets around 45 goals. Barcelona were champions with 99 points and just one defeat. The result would certainly be similar.

In 2010/11 Barcelona moved on both Thierry Henry and Zlatan Ibrahimovic. In our reality they never sign Zlatan and they certainly would not move on the player we signed in his stead, Cristiano Ronaldo. Thierry Henry does move on, so a replacement is needed. In the real timeline Barcelona brought in David Villa. They will do the same in our alternative version.

This brings up interesting possibilities. David Villa played as a central striker for both Spain and Valencia. Guardiola moved him to wide on the left, which is where Ronaldo is playing. Undoubtedly we are forming the Messi, Ronaldo, Villa trio, but how does it shape up? Does Ronaldo make the move to centre-forward early or does Villa play through the middle?

Villa plays through the middle.

It would still be many more years into Ronaldo's career until he developed into a pure centre-forward. David Villa's movement into wide positions would retain a very similar style to that which existed with Henry, except that David Villa would be in his prime, capable of scoring at least 25 goals. Ronaldo would be developing a more selfish and demanding streak. In his second season in Madrid he scored 53 goals in all competitions. For Barcelona he scores around 45. Messi is a prime goal threat. Incredibly, in the real world both players score 53 goals in the 2010/11 season. Messi was already displaying his playmaking qualities; his creative skills come to the fore as he feeds Villa and Ronaldo while also scoring 40 goals of his own.

As time goes on Ronaldo becomes ever more dominant and demanding in front of goal, netting 60 and then 55 goals as the attacking trio play out three seasons, just as Messi, Neymar and Suárez did. Messi is consistently scoring 40 goals a season and racking up the assists while Barcelona utterly dominate La Liga and the Champions League. The accolades and awards keep going to Messi, despite Ronaldo's goals, just as the awards did not go to Suárez or Neymar during their time with Messi. Ronaldo has no Ballon d'Or to his name. He is desperate to win one. After four seasons together Ronaldo calls a halt to proceedings, moving to PSG, just as Neymar would. Collective success could only satisfy these individuals for so long. They rattled up impressive feats of goalscoring and increased their medal collection but Messi leaves

Ronaldo playing catch-up in the individual awards, though Ronaldo now collects more top scorer trophies.

Guardiola's era at Barcelona was defined by intricate beauty. The flowing, fast-paced passing and huge amounts of ball possession, smoothly passing opponents into submission before striking with rapier rapidity within the penalty area. Xavi and Iniesta conducted the orchestra. With Ronaldo on board the two would still be able to conduct, the passing would remain rapid, but there would be some caveats to the way Barcelona play. With Messi in the mix, the pass and move became dribble and move when he received the ball. This is not a comprehensive summary of when Messi had possession, as his passing ability was every bit as extraordinary as his dribbling and scoring in this era, but Messi was more likely to take opponents on than his team-mates. Messi was also more likely to shoot from distance than his team-mates. Ronaldo was renowned for his dribbling but also for his shooting from a variety of angles and positions. Received wisdom would say Ronaldo was selfish because of the volume of shots taken on.

At this relatively early stage in Ronaldo's superstardom he would be more likely to make concessions in his style of play. Barcelona would take on more shots from distance with Ronaldo in the team. Barcelona would attempt more dribbles with Ronaldo in the team. This is not necessarily detrimental. Their possession might drop from 70 per cent to 65 per cent, no disaster.

Similar questions could be asked about Ronaldo's pressing. Barcelona counter-pressed with vigour – this was key to their playing style. Would Ronaldo counter-press? Initially he would. As time passes he might be less willing. This could be where our trio of Messi, Ronaldo and Villa eventually falls down. As Ronaldo's star rises more shots from distance are taken. The pressing is less vigorous. The squabbles over who takes penalties and free kicks grow.

Eventually the town is not big enough for both of them. Ronaldo cannot go to Real Madrid from Barcelona. Spanish football remained too scarred by the Luis Figo incident in the Galactico era. The money of PSG lures him in, just as it did with Neymar. Four seasons of beautiful football, combining the artistry of Messi with the ruthless efficiency of Ronaldo. Glorious imagination finished off with a brutal gut punch. Their time together would be unforgettable and could potentially spark the fire even further. Their relatively silent rivalry has the potential to become a vocal one upon the departure of Ronaldo, with words being exchanged. Ronaldo feeling held back and under-appreciated. Messi feeling Ronaldo's ego had taken over. Winning times could have continued for Barcelona, but Ronaldo was putting personal awards ahead of the club. The rivalry stoked, waiting for the big moment when PSG and Barcelona face off in the Champions League.

Real Madrid would not sit still. They would not simply allow Barcelona to dominate. They would throw money at the problem. Who would they sign? They could make an early move for Neymar, but in 2010 he was only playing his second full season for Santos. Interestingly, Barcelona could still be Neymar's destination once Ronaldo leaves as it would only be a season later than he signs in reality.

The most likely signing for Real Madrid to combat Barcelona's dominance is Zlatan Ibrahimovic. Real Madrid have a historic love for centre-forwards. Zlatan has needed to feel loved and admired. The quantity and consistency of goalscoring from Zlatan at PSG would translate to the quality of supply Real Madrid could provide. Zlatan may not have scored the 450 goals Ronaldo netted for Real, but he would have been a certainty for 300 plus. Zlatan may even have been able to pick up a Ballon d'Or of his own at Madrid. It is wholly likely that if Zlatan stays there for the period Ronaldo did, he would have won a Champions League or two, especially if the Zidane era still occurs.

Rewriting history is not only about what might have happened but also what no longer happens. Certain achievements disappear. Already Ronaldo's legacy suffers by missing out on Ballon d'Or wins. If we further contemplate the way that Messi adapted to playing in the Messi, Suárez, Neymar trio his legacy loses a landmark event. One of Messi's great achievements is his 73-goal season and his 91-goal calendar year. That season and year would fall in the middle of his time with Ronaldo. Messi becoming a more creative force means it is highly likely that these feats would be expunged from the record books.

The two great names remain linked forever, but their relationship and perception are now different. Their story becomes akin to that of classic fiction. Two great friends, partners even, who inspire each other to domination and glory, only for it to come apart and heat up into an epic rivalry. Messi and Ronaldo, eventually squaring off as opponents in a Barcelona vs PSG Champions League Final to decide who truly owns the era.

The great footballing script that was not quite written.

WHAT IF TOM FINNEY HAD BEEN BORN IN A DIFFERENT ERA?

Football is generational. No players are as good as those we saw when we were young and we fell in love with the game. The current debate is whether Messi or Ronaldo is the greatest of all time. Pelé, Di Stéfano and Puskás are all slowly fading from modern memory. The Cruyff 'turn' preserves the great man. Major documentary films have been made about Maradona that thrust him back into the argument. Yet from England, there is a player who so many good judges would bracket alongside all of the above. A player who many think was the greatest footballer that England has ever produced.

Sir Tom Finney was born in Preston in 1922, his generation unlucky enough to come of age just as World War Two was about to rage. From very early it was evident that Finney was born to play football. Even now, watching the stilted images from Pathé News of internationals and cup finals from the 1950s, his speed, balance and athleticism are unmistakable. What differentiates the great players is the ability to maintain this speed and balance with a football at their feet. These elite players seem to have been pre-programmed with the knowledge of football gameplay, to know just where to be at any given time, to know how the football will behave and have complete mastery of it. Finney was genuinely two-footed, could feint both sides, was very quick and had a range of breathtaking tricks with a football that set him apart. His local club Preston wanted to sign him as a professional at 15 years old. He was obviously exceptional, but Finney's father insisted he did a plumbing apprenticeship first. Even at the height of his fame, Finney would be known as the 'Preston Plumber'.

Tom Finney was about to break into the first team at Preston North End when war was declared. He was called up and served in both Egypt and Italy, playing a good deal of football along the way in an army team called 'The Wanderers' that featured many professional and international footballers. The war was no joyride however, and Finney saw a good deal of action in the desert. The footballing gods saw that he made it through without mishap, although he would be 24 when peace was finally established. Despite no professional football having been played for over six years, Finney's reputation as a special player followed him out of the army. He made his debut for Preston in August 1946 and as a full international for England a month later. He had lost six years of his career. To put that into perspective, Wayne Rooney earned 57 caps between the ages of 18 and 24. Finney ended his international career with 76 caps and 30 goals. It's not unreasonable to suggest he would have set records for England that would still not have been broken even now.

What is undeniable is the contribution Finney made to his beloved Preston. Two seasons after his debut he was unable to prevent North End falling into Division Two. They stormed back as champions two years later and remained in the top flight for the rest of Finney's career. Twice they finished runners-up, most frustratingly in 1953 when they lost out to Arsenal only on goal average. In 1954 Finney and Preston reached the FA Cup Final against West Bromwich Albion. He would later admit he was not fully fit and Preston went down 3-2 in one of the more entertaining Wembley finals. Consolation came in the form of the Football Writers' Player of the Year award. Finney won this coveted trophy again in 1957, becoming the first player ever to win it twice. Yet if anything shows how much impact Tom Finney had on the fortunes of Preston North End it is what happened after he retired through a recurring groin injury. At the end of the 1960/61 season Preston were relegated and have never returned to the top flight of English football.

Very few people alive today would have seen Tom Finney play. Football is all about opinion, but some opinions are more equal than others. Revered names from the past rated Finney the best. 'He's arguably the greatest player there has ever been, and I never dreamt that one day I would play with him. An unbelievably gifted footballer,' said Sir Bobby Charlton. Former England manager Roy

Hodgson grew up watching Finney. 'The greatest player this country has ever produced,' he opined. Given the players that both Charlton and Hodgson played with or managed since Finney retired, their opinions have to carry weight. Their views are echoed by so many from that era.

If Finney had been born at another time it is impossible to think he would have been a one-club man. Many of the class of '92 managed that in recent times with Manchester United, but if Finney had broken through at Preston it's likely his path would have been very similar to Wayne Rooney's. Finney would have had a meteoric rise with a season at his local club and then a transfer to one of the giants of English football. If he is bracketed alongside the likes of Pelé and Di Stéfano, which is where his contemporary Stanley Mathews placed him, then it is highly likely he would have gone on to play for one of Europe's elite clubs, such as Barcelona, Real Madrid or Juventus.

So what if Tom Finney was born in a different era?
Finney is born not in 1922 but 1972. When Euro 96 is played in England he is 24 and approaching his peak. He takes the place of Darren Anderton on the left wing in the England line-up. Finney now has Stuart Pearce playing behind him as insurance to allow him to display his full range of skills. He has Paul Gascoigne, another creative genius, to trade passes with, he has Sheringham and Shearer on the end of his crosses.

Under manager Terry Venables England went so close to winning a first major tournament in 20 years. They were solid at the back with captain Tony Adams, Gareth Southgate and newcomer Gary Neville. Paul Ince was probably at his peak here, the midfield 'enforcer' alongside the mercurial Gascoigne. Steve McManaman provided skilful wing play on the right. The partnership of Shearer and Sheringham up front blossomed. England inevitably stuttered at the start of the group games under the weight of expectation, but the 4-1 win against the Netherlands was exhilarating. If Tom Finney, a genuine world-class player is added to this side, it tips the balance from very good to great. He brings out the best in Gascoigne as instinctive footballers often do. Opposition full-backs are wary of pushing forward, knowing Finney is away and gone on the counter. Sheringham and Shearer have a wide variety of Finney crosses to feed on and they create space for Tom to cut inside and score himself. If Tom Finney is born in 1972, Gareth Southgate never takes a penalty, Tony Adams raises the trophy and Terry Venables is knighted.

Finney is born not in 1922 but in 1992. When the 2018 World Cup takes place he is 26. He has experience now added to his considerable talent. He takes the place of Jesse Lingard. Gareth Southgate favours the control of a back three and wing-backs but utilises the world-class Finney now as an inside-forward. Finney has Henderson behind him as a minder and he dominates the midfield with his craft and trickery. His weight of pass plays in the wing-backs Trippier and Young behind the opposition full-backs. He brings out the best in Dele Alli with instinctive one-twos and movement off the ball. Up front he supplies the ammunition to Kane and Sterling, now crossing from deeper, now still making the byline with twinkle-toed feints and tricks to put the ball exactly where the two forwards want it, to head or foot.

In Group G, Finney produces a mesmerising dribble and delicate finish to equalise in a tight game against Belgium, but England still finish second in the group on goal difference. Penalties are not required against Colombia as Finney sets up Kane with a deep cross to the far post and then a tap-in from six yards. Sweden are swept aside and England are in the semi-finals. Against Croatia, England take the lead with Trippier's delicious free kick. Finney takes command of the midfield with probing runs and a range of passes. Just before half-time he plays Kane through centrally; the keeper makes a good save, but the ball breaks back and Finney guides it home through a forest of legs. The Croats pull one back in the second half, but England stand firm and are in their second World Cup Final. France have their glittering line-up, but with Tom Finney in the England side, there is every chance the three lions would now have another star above them.

Anyone born this century would never have seen Zidane or Ronaldo9 at their peak. Their brilliance was already beginning to fade as new heroes took their place. The term 'world-class' is used too liberally. England has produced some truly wonderful players over the years and in 1966 had three that could have been considered 'world-class' in Banks, Moore and Charlton. True footballing genius goes beyond 'world-class'. It defines the 'beautiful game' itself. Like the very best of magic, it fills us with wonder and takes us back to the gleeful joy of our childhood. When football people of the 1950s talk about Tom Finney there is a reverence and an awe, even from those not easily impressed. Bill Shankly played alongside Finney for Preston and managed in an era of outstanding world footballers. 'Tom Finney would have been great in any team, in any match and in any age ... even if he had been wearing an overcoat.'

WHAT IF PELÉ HAD PLAYED IN EUROPE?

'Pelé was one of the few who contradicted my theory: instead of 15 minutes of fame he will have 15 centuries.'

Andy Warhol

As football lovers we take certain things for granted. We assume that laws of the game that we have become accustomed to are common knowledge to all and sundry. That the names famous to us are famous to all. Often when we talk to people with zero interest in football those assumptions are shattered. We mention a player of such esteem as Robert Lewandowski and the face looking back at us is blank. Time also withers the impact of great players, not just on those with no interest in the game, but on those who love the game but have little interest in the history of football. There will be many Liverpool fans with no knowledge of Billy Liddell, Arsenal fans who are unaware of Cliff Bastin.

None of this will ever be the case with Pelé.

People with no interest in football know of Pelé. Young football fans are aware of Pelé. As Warhol implies, the name Pelé will exist forever in the consciousness. He has transcended football and his greatness is accepted by all. In any conversation about the greatest of all time there will be the names of Maradona, Messi, Ronaldo and Pelé.

For good reason. Pelé's achievements in football are astonishing. He played his first match for Santos in Brazil when just 15 years old, scoring in a 7-1 win against Corinthians Santo Andre. His first appearance for Brazil was as a 16-year-old. Aged 17 Pelé was playing in and winning the 1958 World Cup. Pelé scored the only goal for Brazil against Wales in the quarter-final, then a hat-trick against France in the semi-final. The final was against Sweden, with Pelé netting two goals. Six goals in three huge games as a teenager.

At the 1962 World Cup Pelé suffered an injury but Brazil were still able to win the tournament despite him only making two appearances. In 1966 Pelé would also be injured. Brazil roared back with one of the great teams of all time in 1970. Pelé was more mature, an apex 29-year-old who could create as well as score. Pelé scored four goals in the tournament, including the opening goal in the final, Brazil beating Italy 4-1.

There was no Ballon d'Or as we now know it during Pelé's time. The award was only open to European players. *France Football* awarded retrospective Ballon d'Or awards in 2016, giving Pelé the award for 1958, 1959, 1960, 1961, 1963, 1964 and 1970. In the year 2000 the awards rained down on Pelé – World Player of the Century, FIFA Player of the Century, Laureus Lifetime Achievement Award. In retirement Pelé has won almost as many awards as he did while playing.

Pelé's peers held him in the highest regard.

> *'The greatest player in history was Di Stéfano. I refuse to classify Pelé as a player. He was above that.'*
>
> Ferenc Puskás

> *'Pelé was the only footballer who surpassed the boundaries of logic.'*
>
> Johan Cruyff

> *'I told myself before the game, "he's made of skin and bones just like everyone else", but I was wrong.'*
>
> Tarcisio Burgnich, after marking Pelé in the 1970 World Cup Final

Those who played with and against him have little doubt about Pelé's quality and achievements.

One of Pelé's often cited feats is the sheer volume of goals he scored. The magic number is 1,282 but it is this number that is the cause of disputes around the greatness of Pelé. Those who make a case against Pelé's status in the footballing pantheon focus on the legitimacy of the 1,000 goals. They cite that Pelé counted goals scored while playing for the army, goals in friendlies and goals scored on tours.

Tours of Europe by Brazilian teams were very popular and lucrative. Santos first toured in 1959, following on from Brazil's 1958 World Cup success. On that first tour the quality of opponents varied, going from the Bulgarian B team to facing Barcelona in the Nou Camp. Pelé scored twice at the Nou Camp with Santos winning 5-1. They dished out another significant thrashing, beating Inter Milan 7-1.

In 1962 Santos brought their world tour to England. They faced Sheffield Wednesday, who were beaten 4-2 (Pelé scoring a penalty). Santos came back to England in 1969 to play Stoke. Their appearance cost £12,000 and ensured that Pelé would play. He also scored. These tours yielded close to 150 games for Pelé and around 125 goals, precise numbers being unverifiable.

These friendly goals enhance Pelé's case, scoring against the best that Europe could offer; a case further enhanced by the early version of the World Club Cup. The format at that time was that the winners of the European Cup and the winners of the Copa Libertadores faced each other in two games, with two points for a win. Benfica travelled to Brazil to face Santos. Pelé scored twice as Santos won 3-2. The return game in Lisbon finished 5-2 to Santos, Pelé scoring a treble.

Santos defended their Libertadores title and played AC Milan in 1963. Pelé played the first game in Milan, netting twice as Santos lost 4-2. Pelé did not play in the second game, this time won 4-2 by Santos. With the teams level on points a play-off game took place – Santos were the winners but Pelé did not feature in this game either. The seven goals in three games against European champions provides evidence that he was more than capable of prolific scoring against elite teams.

Yet this is not enough for some, who insist that to be rated the greatest ever, Pelé would have to have played in Europe.

What if this had happened? What if Pele had played in Europe?

At the time Brazil's best talents did not populate Europe's top leagues as they do now. Many preferred to stay in Brazil, but there were those who moved.

Brazil's World Cup-winning captain Didi moved to Europe in 1959, joining the star-studded ranks of multi-time European champions Real Madrid. He only stayed for a single season as he and Di Stéfano struggled to co-exist. Another 1958 World Cup winner, José 'Mazzola' Altafini, signed for AC Milan in 1958, playing in Italy until 1976 for AC Milan, Napoli and Juventus. Mazzola naturalised and played half a dozen games for the Italian national team. Other Brazilians were also playing in Italy during the 1960s – Dino da Costa at Fiorentina and Juventus. Jair da Costa at Inter and Roma. Dino Sani at AC Milan. Pelé at Inter Milan.

Almost.

Former owner of Inter Milan, Massimo Moratti, has stated that his father, Angelo, had agreed a deal to sign

Pelé for Inter. The contracts were signed but word had gotten out. The Santos supporters attacked the club and club officials. The deal was cancelled and Pelé remained with Santos until retiring in 1974, then coming back to play for the New York Cosmos a year later.

Had Inter Milan signed Pelé they would have been bringing in a 17-year-old fresh from winning the World Cup with approximately 100 domestic goals to his name. Pelé could have played in Italy until 1974, as Mazzola did. A 16-year career in Italian football, the land of Catenaccio. Surely Pelé, even Pelé, could not have scored the same volume of goals?

Inter Milan and Helenio Herrera were key implementors of Catenaccio. Two European Cups were won, in 1964 and 1965, with their defence-first mindset. AC Milan had won the European Cup in 1963 playing a slightly more attacking form of Catenaccio. This defensive style did not prevent players scoring high numbers of goals in Serie A. John Charles scored 28 goals as top scorer in 1957/58. Antonio Valentín Angelillo scored 33 goals in 1958/59. Omar Sívori scored 28 in 1959/60. The top scorer consistently netted over 20 goals a season. Though this is far off the 40-, 50- and even 60-goal totals Pelé scored in Brazil, these are still impressive goal totals.

The Inter Milan manager in 1958 was Giuseppe Bigogno. This was a turbulent period for Inter, with five managers between 1958 and 1960, when they appointed Helenio Herrera. Herrera had already experienced a successful decade managing in Spain, winning La Liga with Atletico Madrid in 1949/50 and again in 1950/51. In 1958 he found himself at the Nou Camp, once more winning back-to-back La Liga titles. In Spain, Herrera's teams played an attacking style, scoring heavily. Barcelona scored 96 goals in 30 games in 1958/59 and 86 goals in 1959/60. The formation used was a 2-3-2-3, though most systems of the time were labelled in the manner, as some form of W-M shape. Hungarian forwards Czibor and Kubala were key, with Spaniard Luis Suárez (not that one) the heart of the team.

Herrera started with the same attacking style at Inter. The team scored 73 goals in 39 games, conceding 39. However, one result would put an end to this. In the final game of the season Juventus scored nine times against Inter. Forward Omar Sívori grabbed six goals. Herrera tightened up defensively and deployed man-marking and a sweeper. The goals scored and conceded initially decreased but eventually the scoring improved. By 1964/65 Inter were scoring two goals per game in Serie A, finishing with 16 goals more than the next highest scoring team. The following season Inter scored even more, with 70 goals in their 34 games.

Fast vertical football was the Herrera style. Counter-attacking rapidly. Herrera was insistent that everyone who copied his Catenaccio simply forgot to attack, pointing out that in his teams goals came from all positions, using attacking full-backs like Giacinto Facchetti, a scorer of double-figure goal totals from left-back. Suárez also joined Inter from Barcelona, becoming their key playmaker.

Pelé would not have lacked scoring opportunities. He showed on many occasions that he was capable of scoring against top European opponents. The barrier to him scoring goals in such vast numbers may have simply been opportunity. Pelé would not have been able to play in so many tour games and friendlies to build his goal total. He would have had 34 Serie A games a year, a handful of Coppa Italia games and at most nine European Cup games. If Pelé is fit and appears in every game he plays fewer than 50 matches in an average season. The European Cup would afford opportunities for heavy goalscoring in the early rounds, where Pelé could pick off opponents and bolster his scoring.

To get an idea of how Pelé might perform we can look at his contemporaries. Eusébio's goalscoring reputation is similar to that of Pelé, but the Portuguese league played far fewer games than anyone else. In Europe, for a hugely successful Benfica, Eusébio's record was 57 goals in 75 games. Gerd Müller, playing for Bayern Munich in a similar era, scored 65 goals in 74 games. It would be fair to suggest that between 1958 and 1974 Pelé would have been able to score over 60 goals in European competition.

In Serie A Pelé is playing in almost the exact same time period as José 'Mazzola' Altafini but spends his whole career at a much more successful team. Altafani played 459 Serie A games, scoring 216 goals playing as a striker and wide player. Altafani also had injury-hit seasons. Sandro Mazzola was a key player at Inter during this time period, playing in an attacking role. His career numbers are 418 games and 116 goals. Jair da Costa played right-wing for Inter from 1962–67 and played 119 games, scoring 39 goals. It would seem that in that era the best players scored at a goal every two games to a goal every three games. They would have seasons when they managed close to a goal a game but could not maintain it for their whole career.

However, Pelé was not one of the best players, he was *the* best player. In 16 seasons he would play approximately 480 games (at 30 Serie A games a season, allowing for injuries here and there). It is quite conceivable that he scores 400 goals. It is equally conceivable that he does better than that, scoring even closer to a goal a game. If Pelé scores 450 goals in Serie A, 60 in Europe and 30 in the Coppa Italia his total for Inter is 540 goals. Add on the 77 goals he has for Brazil and the 100 goals he scored in Brazil before leaving, then Pelé ends his career with over 700 goals, with no friendly or tour games included. An incredible total but equally incredibly, 500 goals fewer than his mythical 1,200-plus goal figure.

How would Pelé being at Inter Milan impact them and Italian football? In the late 1950s managers changed constantly and the club was unstable; it is unlikely that situation would change. Fortunes would not improve until Herrera is appointed in 1960. The first season's goal total of 73 would likely be higher with Pelé in the team, but he would not have any impact on the team defensively. This Herrera tightens up at the back.

In 1961/62 Inter finished second to AC Milan, five points behind. Inter and AC Milan both lost just five games, but Inter drew five more. In this era of two points for a win and one for a draw those draws were less damaging than they would be under three points for a win. Pelé would boost the goal total but might not be able to turn enough of those draws into wins.

In 1962/63 Inter are champions, four points ahead of Juventus. The defence dominates, only conceding 20 goals in 34 games. Inter's goals are shared around, with multiple players scoring double figures. Inter only scored 56 goals that season, but Pelé would surely boost that total and score close to 20 goals himself.

The following season Inter finish level on points with Bologna, who are crowned Serie A champions on goal difference. In the head-to-head results Inter beat Bologna 2-1 away but drew 0-0 at home. A single Pelé goal and the title swings to Inter, adding the league title to their European Cup win. The final was a 3-1 win over Real Madrid. Pelé scoring in that game adds another positive mark to his legacy.

In 1964/65 Inter Milan won the Intercontinental Cup, the European Cup and Serie A. This would mean consecutive Serie A and European Cup doubles for Inter.

In Serie A they scored two goals a game without Pelé. They would likely score many more with him and this would be an opportunity for Pelé to have a huge scoring season of over 30 goals in Serie A. Inter beat Benfica 1-0 in the final, Pelé's compatriot Jair scored the only goal.

Inter score 70 goals to win Serie A in 1965/66. This is another opportunity for Pelé to have a 30-plus goal season. This would be four consecutive Serie A titles for *I Nerazzurri*. In Europe Real Madrid squeeze Inter out two goals to one over two legs. Could Pelé have found a goal to beat Real Madrid? Had he done so then Inter would surely go on to beat Partizan Belgrade in the final as Real did. Pelé, Inter and Herrera now have four straight Serie A wins and three successive European Cups.

Juventus edge Inter by a single point in 1966/67. Inter drop points in a 1-1 draw at home to Juventus. They lose 1-0 in Turin as they collapse at the end of the season. The three games after losing to Juventus are a 1-1 draw at home to Napoli, a 1-1 draw at home to Fiorentina and 1-0 loss at Mantova. One Pelé goal in any of these five games would be enough to crown Inter champions for a fifth season in a row.

In the European Cup, Inter Milan reach the final against Celtic. Famously a Celtic team assembled of local boys beat them 2-1. Inter went ahead early but sat back for the rest of the game, allowing Celtic back into the contest. With Pelé in their ranks it would have been much harder for Celtic to cope. It took Celtic over an hour to equalise and their winner came with just six minutes to go – could Pelé have scored during that period? This would give Inter a 2-1 win and erase Celtic as the first ever British European Cup winners. Inter would now have five straight Serie A wins and four European Cups in a row. This level of success in Europe, plus two World Cups, would erase most of the question marks against Pelé by the time he is 26 years old. The World Cup win in 1970 put his greatness beyond any doubt.

The Herrera era imploded dramatically in 1968, with Inter falling down to fifth in Serie A. Even Pelé's brilliance would not be able to turn the turmoil into a title. Pelé would continue to score but Inter would enter a transitional period after unparalleled success. In 1969 they appointed another Herrera, Heriberto. Heriberto had won Serie A with Juventus and took Inter to second in 1970. He was removed as Inter manager after a poor start to the 1970/71 season. His replacement, Giovanni Invernizzi, rejuvenated the squad. Having lost to Napoli in the seventh league game of the campaign Inter would be unbeaten for the rest of the season and win Serie A. Pelé would have another title to his name and another tilt at the European Cup.

The Invernizzi revival would not last in Serie A as Inter dropped down to fifth place, but he did take *I Nerazzurri* to another European Cup Final. Here we would have the intriguing prospect of Inter and Pelé versus Ajax and Cruyff. This was the second of the Dutch club's famous three wins in a row, taking place in Rotterdam, giving Ajax the home nation advantage. The actual game finished 2-0 with Cruyff scoring twice. Cruyff was 25 years old and entering the peak of his powers. Pelé would be 31, a three-time World Cup winner and four-time European champion. The young lion versus the old lion, a classic tale as old as time. Could Pelé find one more piece of brilliance against the team of the moment and total football? Pelé may have found a moment of magic but it is unlikely to have changed the result as Ajax were that irresistible at the time, but Pelé could have helped Inter put up more of a fight and his mere presence and legacy would have enhanced the reputation of Ajax and Cruyff, dethroning the greatest player and one of the greatest teams.

Pelé retires in 1974 after Inter have two relatively limp seasons, with fifth- and fourth-place finishes. Having spent so long at the very top of European football his reputation and achievements are undeniable. There are no doubts, no questions to answer on the matter of his greatness.

WHAT IF BRAZIL 1970
PLAYED SPAIN 2008–12?

What is the greatest football team of all time?

People delight in absolutes and having heated but ultimately pointless debates about the word 'greatest'. A wonderful way to spend an afternoon with friends.

The discussion will inevitably split between club and international teams. Equally inevitably, Brazil 1970 will be brought up. If we were to pick a marquee international fixture to decide the greatest team of all time, Brazil 1970 would undoubtedly be involved.

For a generation the 1970 FIFA World Cup was the most important and most eye-opening event. It was the first tournament broadcast in colour, which immediately provided added vibrancy. England went into the tournament as defending world champions, decked out in an iconic, pure, all-white kit. Then there was the mystique and magic of Brazil, whose distinct bright yellow shirts came to polychromatic life.

Brazil offered an irresistible cocktail for the global audience, the primary attraction being a global legend at the apex of his career, Pelé. At the 1958 World Cup

Pelé made a huge impact as a teenager. In 1962 he was injured early on in the tournament, Brazil victorious despite his absence. In 1966 Pelé received notoriously rough treatment from opponents, with injury hampering his involvement and Brazil's progress. By 1970 Pelé had a point to prove.

The Brazil squad was packed with attacking talent. As well as Pelé the line-up featured Tostão, Jairzinho, Gerson, Rivellino and Clodoaldo. The team was captained by Carlos Alberto, an aggressive, attacking right-back. Brazil played six games at the tournament, winning all six. In the group stage Brazil cruised past Czechoslovakia 4-1 before facing England. The defending champions would be beaten 1-0 in a game laced with iconic moments. That tackle by Moore. What a save by Gordon Banks! Jeff Astle fizzing a low, left-footed chance a fraction wide with the score still 0-0. Jairzinho ripping a shot into the net following a Pelé assist. Bobby Moore and Pelé embracing at the end of the game.

Brazil then beat Romania 3-2 in their final group game. Next was Peru 4-2 in the quarter-final. Uruguay 3-1 in the semi-final. They provided further iconic moments as they progressed to the final with spectacular swerving free kicks and dazzling skills but Pelé was creating his own personal highlight reel. As well as scoring the goals he was creating them. Yet it was the almost moments that resounded most. Almost scoring from halfway. Almost scoring after an outrageous dummy, leaving a long through ball then running round a bamboozled goalkeeper, the shot from a tight angle trundling just wide. Slamming a miscued goal kick immediately back at goal.

In the final Brazil met the notoriously outstanding Italian defence. The glorious passing of Gerson, dazzling dribbling of Rivellino, thunderous shooting of Tostão and hunger for goals of Jairzinho were far too much for Italy. Pelé opened the scoring with a gravity-defying leap and pneumatic pump of the neck muscles. The final goal of the game is one of the most iconic goals in football history. A sweeping team move capped with Pelé's glorious lay-off to Carlos Alberto, made all the more memorable because Pelé appears to pass into a completely empty space until Carlos Alberto gallops into the frame and lashes a right-foot shot into the corner. The game is won 4-1. This is the measuring stick for all Brazilian teams that have followed them.

Who would they face off against though? In over 100 years of internationals football has witnessed many fantastic teams. How do we select and define their greatness?

The team has to have two features. It has to have won a major trophy and enchant the imagination in some way. Numerous teams fulfil one of these but not many secure both. Greece were successful but were the antithesis of enchanting. Hungary 1954, Netherlands 1974 and Brazil 1982 enchanted but failed to bring home the trophy, so they are out.

Brazil have had many great teams, with the 1958–62 side strong contenders, but I am not convinced anyone really wants to watch Brazil vs Brazil. Besides, Pelé would really struggle to play for both 1958–62 and 1970 at the same time. None of the West German or German teams have captured the imagination. The same can be said of Italy. France from 1998–2000 are very strong contenders with a mix of wonderful individuals, fine football and trophy wins. However, using the criteria there is a group better suited to the task.

Spain did not quite have the individual flair of Brazil 1970 in any of their three great teams. They were true teams. In 2008 the first task of Luis Aragonés was to bring together the rival Real Madrid and Barcelona players. In 2008 Barcelona were pre-Guardiola and Spain pre- the tiki-taka brand of football. Their style was somewhat more direct than they would become but the keys to the performances were the talents in midfield, something that would only become increasingly important across the coming tournaments. An axis of Xavi and Iniesta was cemented, with Fernando Torres the spearhead as the sole striker. David Villa was a key to the team, playing as a second striker but with the freedom to drift across the pitch. However, his tournament was cut short by an injury, leaving Torres isolated in the final. However, that glorious isolation would lead to the only goal of the 2008 European Championship Final – Torres sprinting on to a Xavi through-ball to dink a finish over the advancing goalkeeper.

By 2010 Spain had developed further, now managed by Vicente del Bosque and heavily under the stylistic influence of Pep Guardiola. Spain's possession football was criticised at times for lacking a cutting edge and they opened the tournament with a 1-0 loss against Switzerland. From there they won every game but scored few goals. In the group stage they scored twice to beat Honduras and then beat Chile 2-1. From the last 16 through to the final all of their games were won by the scoreline of 1-0. By now the defence was well established: Iker Casillas in goal, Sergio Ramos at right-back, Carles Puyol and Gerard Piqué as the central defenders and Juan Capdevila at left-back. The midfield was the Spanish powerhouse. Sergio Busquets, Xabi Alonso, Andrés Iniesta and Xavi were the core. Xavi and Iniesta are synonymous as a central midfield paring but Iniesta was used as a wide player by Spain. Such was the midfield depth that David Silva, Juan Mata and Cesc Fàbregas were substitutes. It was from the bench that Fàbregas slipped a killer pass to Iniesta to stroke in the only goal of the final versus a rough, tough Netherlands team.

In 2012 Spain were in their final, apex form. The tiki-taka style had fully embedded into the team and the side played mostly without a centre-forward, using Cesc Fàbregas in the false nine role, dropping from a traditional centre-forward position into deeper midfield areas. Torres came off the bench to play as a more traditional forward but in the final against Italy they started with six players who could be classified as playing in central midfield roles: Andrés Iniesta, Xavi, Sergio Busquets, David Silva, Xabi Alonso and Cesc Fàbregas. This relied on players making forward runs from deeper and wider positions. If the runs did not come or the passes were not picked out Spain could become turgid, as they were in the semi-final against Portugal, drawing 0-0 and only coming through after a penalty shoot-out. However, when it clicked into gear the style was fluid, exciting and impossible to stop. This was the case in the final as Spain produced a wonderful show of fast passing and off-the-ball movement to win 4-0.

We have our teams for this fantasy match-up – now we must make a few adjustments to set the scene fully. For Brazil the team squad and manager are clear and straightforward. For Spain, spanning three tournaments, it is less transparent. In terms of manager we will take Del Bosque as he won two of the three trophies and coached the Spanish side when they performed in the manner that most would associate with them. The high-possession, counter-pressing style adapted from Guardiola's Barcelona was most apparent in 2012, therefore the majority of the team will be that 2012 line-up. A few changes should be made. Ramos should be moved from his 2012 central defender position to his 2010 and 2008 right-back position. This makes room for Carles Puyol. Capdevila played in both the 2008 and 2010 finals but Jordi Alba's overlapping runs are so key to the style of the 2012 team, he gets the start. Switching Puyol in does not impact the playing style to the same extent. In the forward positions David Villa takes one of the spaces. He comes in for David Silva, moving to the left side of an extremely narrow midfield. Iniesta has to shift across to the right. Fàbregas remains as a false nine.

We will assume that Brazil have adopted modern fitness methods and neither team will have a physical advantage. The game requires a neutral venue. We will select Wembley Stadium, but not the new Wembley topped with a metallic arch, but the Wembley with the Twin Towers. A ball should also be selected, given footballs have changed a great deal over time, a ball from a neutral time period would be suitable. The Italia 90 World Cup is 20 years after Brazil's win and 20 years before Spain's. The ball for the game will be the Adidas Etrusco Unico from the 1990 tournament.

What we cannot do is give Brazil modern tactics. They can only use the tactics they displayed in 1970. Similarly, Spain will only use the 2012 tactics. While the 2008 team would sling in crosses this was rare for the 2012 side. Spain will be using a short passing style.

The Spanish team of 2008 had more in common with Manuel Pellegrini's Real Madrid in terms of formation. The system was a highly flexible 4-2-3-1 that morphed into 4-2-4 or 4-2-2-2. The team set up in a mid-block, looking for opportunities to regain the ball close to the halfway line rather than being committed to applying pressure close to the opponent's penalty area in a high press. By 2010 this had changed – the system was 4-2-3-1, built upon a triangular axis of Xavi, Busquets and Xabi Alonso. All three were capable of acting as playmakers, while Busquets could drop into the defensive line when required.

This triangle remained in place by 2012. In 2010 David Villa was a clear striker for the Spanish side. By 2012 he had signed for Barcelona and played wide on the left. Spain used him there before his injury in the early stages. Cesc Fàbregas played as a false nine, with Andrés Iniesta wide. This is the system that will face Brazil. One built around a narrow midfield, packed with possession experts who make clever runs in behind defences, the spaces for these runs created by the movement of the false nine, dragging central defenders out of position. The narrow formation relied on clever midfielders pulling wide (Silva or Iniesta) or the full-backs overlapping aggressively (Alba and Arbeloa in 2012, Ramos in our line-up).

Possession for Spain had multiple purposes. To control the tempo of the game. To allow players to conserve energy and tire out the opposition. To prevent the opposition from scoring. To pull opponents out of position. Possession was the key, thus at restarts Spain would use their goal kicks to pass the ball short and start the passing cycle all over again.

Spain were the epitome of system and team; their reward was three consecutive tournament victories.

Brazil were the masters of individuality and finding ways for their elite talents to flourish.

Tactically Brazil were sophisticated if not complicated. Defensively the team sat off in a somewhat passive deep block, not really looking to regain the ball until it had progressed deep inside their territory. Central defenders Brito and Piazza stayed deep, with left-back Everaldo not straying too far forward. Right-back Carlos Alberto provided attacking thrust on the right-hand side of the back four.

The shape ahead of the back four is often characterised as a 'Brazilian box', a 4-2-2-2 with two players sitting deep, two as attacking midfielders and two strikers, but the system was far more fluid and flexible than that. Clodoaldo generally remained closer to the back four, playing shorter, connecting passes. Gerson performed a playmaking role, spraying longer passes and using his long-range shooting ability. The brilliant dribbler Rivellino largely stuck to the left-hand side but would tuck inside behind the forwards, into a number ten position.

It is the relationship between Pelé, Tostão and Jairzinho where the sophistication emerges. Jairzinho played nominally as a right-winger, but he had licence to arrive in the centre-forward position. This was possible because both Pelé and Tostão had total freedom to take up any position on the pitch, pulling away from the centre-forward role, creating space for Tostão to arrive into. Pelé spent much of the tournament dropping deep, rather than running in

behind – Jairzinho did the running in behind. Pelé then got into the box when the ball was in wide areas to exploit his heading ability. The Brazilian attack functioned much in the way we would consider the relationship between a false nine and modern goalscoring wide men.

With the tactical approaches clear, just how does our game play out?

Brazil's start is as bright as their shimmering yellow strip. They have early possession with Gerson spraying passes from flank to flank. One switch of play picks out Rivellino on the left. He tricks a couple of defenders, slithering into the penalty area. His thunderous left-boot strike is brilliantly fingertipped on to the post by Iker Casillas.

Spain's possession and technical football is much discussed but far less discussed is that in goal they had a match-winner. At times Real Madrid were porous defensively but Casillas pulled off remarkable saves to keep the opposition at bay. Spain's defending was far better but Iker still possessed the same match-winning capabilities.

The tempo of the game settles down. Brazil keep their distance from Spain, who stroke the ball around. They are happy to keep possession and unwilling to take risks early in the game. Possession without penetration, almost sterile football.

Brazil pinch possession in the centre of the pitch through Clodoaldo. He passes short to Tostão, who sets the ball back to Gerson. Jairzinho begins his run in behind and Gerson picks him out. Jairzinho's touch takes him a fraction too wide to shoot so he clips a ball back towards the penalty spot. Pelé leaps and powers a header down and into the bottom corner beyond the dive of Casillas. Brazil take the lead inside the first quarter of an hour.

Spain crank things up a gear. They begin to counter-press with more ferocity, regaining possession frequently. Their probing passes force some desperate Brazilian defending leading to corner kicks, but Brazil scramble them away. Just.

Brito finally gets sucked in by Fàbregas' movement. Fàbregas drops short and receives the ball. Brito follows him, leaving a gap in the Brazilian back line. Fàbregas passes to Xavi, who lays the ball off to Xabi Alonso. Alonso punches a pass into the gap vacated by Brito. David Villa races on to it. As he strikes the shot Carlos Alberto recovers brilliantly, deflecting the shot on to the bar and behind for a corner.

There are mere moments before half-time. Alonso fizzes a corner into the near post area, and Sergio Ramos, master of the big goal, adds another to his collection, flicking the ball into the roof of net. Half-time and the scores are level.

The pattern of the second half is one of Spanish possession punctuated by Brazilian breakaways. Now that Spain are level they have returned to risk-averse mode. Slowly passing higher and higher up the pitch. Pushing Brazil further back. By the midway point of the second half Spain's central defenders are camped almost 15 yards inside the Brazil half. This leaves acres of space behind the Spanish defence with Brazil poised to break.

Pelé pounces on a stray pass and sets Jairzinho away. Puyol struggles to keep up and brings Jairzinho down 35 yards out. Controversially, he escapes with only a yellow card. It seems like half of the Brazil team are interested in taking the free kick. Eventually they back away, leaving Tostão, Pelé and Rivellino. Tostão unleashes a swerving effort, dipping late and flicking off the top of the Spanish crossbar.

Inside the last ten minutes Spain have been unable to create a real chance despite having almost 70 per cent of possession. Brazil have held firm but when they lose the ball in their own half Spain press the Brazilian defenders hard. They have to be more cautious when the midfielders regain possession because their technical ability enables them to play through the press on a number of occasions, Casillas having to be alert and sweep up the danger.

Finally, Xavi flicks a pass into the Brazilian penalty area. Iniesta times his run perfectly. For the first time Spain have a runner from midfield and Iniesta controls the ball perfectly with the laces of his right foot. Almost instantly he pokes the ball through the legs of the onrushing Felix. Spain take the lead, 2-1 with five minutes remaining.

Brazil dig deep. In stoppage time Tostão finds Pelé on the edge of the Spanish penalty area. He shimmies and twists. Casillas is fractionally off his line. Of course, the master has spotted this. Pelé floats a chipped effort goalward. Casillas is stranded, an onlooker just like everyone else as the ball drifts towards goal ... and it keeps drifting a fraction wide of the post.

Spain have won 2-1, ultimately starving Brazil of enough of the ball for their individuals to do too much damage. Victory for the team over the individuals, but it was mighty close.

WHAT IF PEP GUARDIOLA MANAGED IN LEAGUE TWO?

Pep Guardiola divides the opinion of many football fans. Some see him as one of the most innovative coaches of his generation, his teams playing breathtaking football and taking control of the game to another level. For others he is a cheque book manager who also inherits great players and would never have achieved his success without the backing of billions.

What is often overlooked is that Guardiola did not end his playing days and walk straight into the Barcelona dressing room as first-team coach. Guardiola was always a student of the game. In the Barcelona 'Dream Team' of the early 1990s, fashioned by Johan Cruyff, his role was that of the central pivot. He dictated the pace and the rhythm of the team's passing so that the stars like Stoichkov and Laudrup could work their magic. After 17 years playing for Barcelona he went to sample a different style of football in Italy with Brescia, taking over from another famous *regista*, Andrea Pirlo. There followed a spell in Qatar, but with several English Premier League teams chasing his signature, Guardiola took a pilgrimage

79

to Mexico to play for Dorados de Sinaloa. The manager there, Juan Manuel Lillo, helped to shape Guardiola's future coaching. In 2020 Lillo followed his former pupil to Manchester City, becoming assistant manager to Guardiola. It was while in Mexico that Guardiola sought out one of football's coaching gurus, Marcelo Bielsa. After travelling thousands of miles to meet with Bielsa, Guardiola spent many hours talking football and coaching with the great man. There is no doubt that this legendary meeting came to shape the philosophy that would make Guardiola renowned within the game.

In 2007, the year after Guardiola retires as a player, he takes up a position as coach of Barcelona B who play in the Segunda Division B, the third tier of Spanish football. The team achieve promotion via the play-offs in Guardiola's first ever season as a coach. There is no cheque book to wave here. He has good young technical players, but Guardiola achieves everything through his innovative coaching. With Frank Rijkaard struggling with Barcelona's first team, and amidst undoubted controversy, Pep Guardiola is appointed manager of Barcelona. In his first full season as a first-team coach, Guardiola wins La Liga and the Copa del Rey, and becomes the youngest coach ever to win the Champions League. In four years he wins 14 trophies. After a year's sabbatical, Guardiola returns to football with Bayern Munich where he wins five trophies in three years. In 2016 he makes his much-anticipated move to Manchester City, starting work again under Txiki Begiristain and Ferran Soriano, two men instrumental in taking the risk with Guardiola to give him his first managerial job at Barcelona. Their reward has not only been a haul of trophies, but to reset many of the English Premier League records, including 100 points in a single season.

Guardiola's record in management is unquestionably remarkable, but he has worked for two of the biggest clubs in world football and taken Manchester City closer to the elite. 'Anyone could do what Guardiola has done with all the billions he has spent on players. Let's see him do it in League Two!' cry his critics.

So, what happens if Guardiola does not take up his position at Barcelona B in 2007? What if he is on holiday and meets the ambitious new owner of an English League Two club who offers him an opportunity?

What if Pep Guardiola's first steps in management are in England in League 2?

Pep Guardiola accepts the invitation of Barry, the ambitious new owner of Oldale, to become first-team manager for the start of the 2007/08 League Two season. Oldale were once in the Championship and Barry believes Guardiola is the man to return the club 'to where it belongs'. There is no real budget to spend on players, but Barry is a keen follower of football and has it on good authority from people in the game that Pep is a 'coach to watch'. There is no real budget to spend on staff either. Many have been with the club for years. Pep is allowed to bring in an assistant manager. He asks for an analyst, a dietician, a fitness coach and a physio. Barry says he can have one of the three. Pep brings with him from Spain his fitness coach. Jim, the long-standing fitness and physio man at Oldale leaves the club, telling the press, 'All this fancy Dan stuff from Spain won't work in English football.'

The players return for their pre-season. Pep tells them everyone will start with a clean slate, everyone will be judged equally in the first weeks. 'What I can promise is that I will not tolerate lack of effort.' The old pros are taken aback that their first sessions do not involve running, running and more running. They start with position games, tactical games and passing exercises, all at high intensity. Some players thrive. Others struggle. At the end of the first week, Lee, the club's top scorer and fans' favourite, Gary the club captain and Eddie the first-choice keeper are told they will not feature in Pep's plans. The fans are not happy. Barry has to hold his nerve. Lee is replaced by Aiden on loan from Manchester United, a slight 18-year-old who is quick. Sir Alex trusts Pep to 'look after him'. Chelsea also loan one of their promising full-backs, Jay.

Pep is the first to arrive and the last to leave every day. He takes a great interest in the Oldale youth team. It has produced some good young talent in the past. After watching them play in a friendly, Pep promotes three of the youngsters to train with the first team. Pre-season training gathers pace. There are fines for lateness, there are fines for being overweight, and the fines are not going to the 'Lads' Christmas Party', but to charity. Oldale is being changed from top to bottom. But Pep is getting buy-in from the squad. The sessions are intense, but fun. The young players are pushing the seasoned pros. Pep meets with the club's official supporters' group. All of the first-team squad attend. Pep insists they stop and sign autographs for as long as is necessary. Barry tells the fans they are in for something special.

Until the season kicks off. Then Oldale are two goals down to newly promoted Morecambe in 20 minutes. Morecambe go long and pump balls into the box. Pep's decision to play former midfielder Jimmy at centre-half seems to backfire as his lack of height from corners and set pieces make Oldale vulnerable. At half-time Pep tells the players to believe in what they are doing. They rally in the second half to draw level, but with ten minutes to go, rookie keeper Callum kicks badly as he tries to play out short. Oldale lose 3-2.

After six games Oldale are in the bottom three. They haven't won a game, drawing two and losing four, including a 5-0 humiliation away to Grimsby on a wet Tuesday. Barry is getting nervous. Pep calls the players in for a meeting. He holds his hands up and says he has made mistakes. While fans' favourite Lee and keeper Eddie have left, Pep has been very impressed by the way former club captain Gary has knuckled down and trained hard. Pep has decided that 3-4-3 is not really working for the team. He is going to change to a 4-3-3 formation. He still wants his team to control possession and play out from the back, he still wants to the full-backs to join in midfield and the wingers to hug the touchlines. He believes in his players. After some frank exchanges, he gets what he wants – total commitment to the cause.

The next game is away to Peterborough who have been flying. With just two minutes to go, Oldale are winning 2-1 and Aiden has scored them both, but they concede from a corner. The result means they are now bottom of League Two. Even so it is a turning point. Oldale were much the better side. Pep is very pleased with the performance. The fans are divided. Why is Pep playing a midfielder at centre-half? Why is the right-winger on the left and the left-winger on the right? Why has he not signed a centre-forward? And anyone can see the full-backs leave gaps when they move inside. But after Peterborough, Oldale go on a five-match unbeaten run. They are starting to control games. 'I want every move to be smart, every pass to be accurate – that's how we make a difference from the rest of the teams – that's all I want to see.' The run comes to an end when Oldale travel to table-topping MK Dons and face their old boy Lee. After a pulsating game with chances at both ends Lee scores the inevitable winner with five minutes to go. Lee celebrates wildly in front of the Oldale dugout. Pep wishes him well for the season in the press conference after. Things get worse for

Oldale. Box-to-box midfielder Carlton has suffered a knee ligament injury and will be out for months.

Pep's solution to the Carlton crisis is to promote teenage left-back Donny from the youth team. His fitness coach has shown Pep the numbers from Donny's training sessions. His overlapping and recovery runs are impressive. He can pass the ball too. Pep decides he will try him as his number eight.

It's a hunch that works like a dream. In tandem with Gary there is great energy in the midfield. Oldale are pressing and winning the ball more in their opposition half. In the next ten games they lose only once, away at Stockport. By Christmas they are hovering just under the play-off positions.

Pep wants to save the big party until the end of the season. Barry persuades him it is an Oldale tradition for the boys to let their hair down at Christmas. Pep has never had to play four games in so short a time. The festive period does not go well. Two draws and two defeats see Oldale lose ground again. Pep decides to freshen up the squad and signs jet-heeled wide-man Michael from Arsenal's youth squad. He also picks up 30-year-old centre-half Bob from League One side Tranmere. Bob was with Everton as a kid and has two caps for England under-21s. He's lost a yard of pace, but he can play. Pep loves his leadership. During a game, Bob never shuts up.

January sees Oldale drawn away to Coventry in the third round of the FA Cup. Oldale take a shock early lead and an upset looks on the cards before Coventry come back strong with three goals in the last 15 minutes. Pep locks the team in the dressing room after the game. He tells them this is exactly how he wants the team to play, to be brave on the ball, to control, to attack and to believe they can win any game.

Pep redoubles his own efforts. 'It was as if he was a vastly experienced coach who was going to be facing Milan, Madrid and Bayern every week,' says Barry. 'His attention to detail when he assesses our opponents is amazing.' The detail begins to pay off. Oldale go on a 15-match unbeaten run that includes wins against their fellow play-off hopefuls Wycombe, Rotherham and Chesterfield. They hold MK Dons to a 0-0 draw at home. Much to the delight of the home fans, young keeper Callum saves a penalty from their old hero Lee. Aiden has now scored 24 league goals. The scouts are gathering. Alex Ferguson has been down to check.

With four games to go, Oldale are in the play-off positions, but they lose two games on the run, away at Hereford and at home to bogey side Grimsby. The final game of the league season arrives. If Oldale beat Bury at home they are in the play-offs. They win comfortably, 3-1. Pep keeps everyone's feet on the ground. 'We have done nothing yet.' Barry buys a new suit for Wembley. Oldale beat Darlington in the play-off semi-finals first leg 1-0. With such a slender lead, their control and temperament in the second leg is impressive. There are just five minutes remaining when Gary scores the decisive goal to kill the tie. He runs straight over to Pep. The whole team piles on.

Guardiola's preparation for the Division Two play-off final against Wycombe is immaculate. He organises the travel, the hotel, the route to Wembley, and the time with the press. The players are bouncing in training. Pep arranges a night with the fans with the whole first-team squad there. Oldale take over 15,000 fans to Wembley, more than double their average matchday attendance. In the run up to kick-off he spends individual time with each player, he runs through every set play, and then finishes with a final call to arms. The team are ready. Barry is sitting in the Royal Box proudly telling everyone he 'discovered Guardiola'. The teams line up. Pep Guardiola leads Oldale out at Wembley, his first return since the 1992 European Cup Final.

There are a number of coaches who have shown that it is possible to bounce a team through the divisions, most notably Eddie Howe with Bournemouth. Good coaching in the lower tiers does make a difference. If Pep Guardiola takes Oldale up to League One, if they maintain their momentum there is every chance he is offered a job at one of the sleeping giants like Leicester or Southampton who were in the third tier of English football around this time. What if he is successful with a club like this, taking them into the Premier League, finishing high enough to qualify for the UEFA Cup, picking up an FA Cup or a League Cup along the way, and finally finishing fourth and claiming a Champions League spot? If this happens by the end of season 2013, there is every chance that Pep Guardiola takes over from Sir Alex Ferguson, so that he reaches the pinnacle of English football not with Manchester City, but with Manchester United.

WHAT IF ENGLAND HAD BUILT THEIR TEAM AROUND GLENN HODDLE?

If you were told that the most talented player of a generation had a nine-year international career, during which he only won 53 caps, you might be surprised. However, you might be less surprised if you were told his nation was England.

Historically English football has systematically failed to get the best out of technically excellent, creative and imaginative players. The 1970s, 80s and 90s were eras of wasted international talent. For decades it seemed like managers did not know how to use a specific type of player, nor did they seem to feel that they could rely on them.

Chris Waddle and John Barnes seemed to be distrusted by a series of England managers, but they were relatively lucky, earning 62 and 79 caps, wingers getting a little bit of leeway. How else could England get the delivery into their conveyor belt of big centre-forwards?

Central midfielders were particularly poorly treated. If you play a rigid 4-4-2 with a big man and little man strike partnership, how can you fit in an attack-minded central midfielder? Let alone a creative number 10?

Three players have been particularly mismanaged. Paul Gascoigne, who only gained 57 England caps. For Gazza there were personal circumstances that prevented him from having a fully formed international career. Paul Scholes, who only earned 66 international caps, at a time when his midfield contemporaries Gerrard and Lampard soared past 100. Scholes was a victim of the 4-4-2. Glenn Hoddle, who only earned 53 international caps, a victim of 4-4-2, mistrust, and misunderstanding.

Hoddle made his Tottenham Hotspur debut in 1975 aged just 17. The next season he played 39 top-flight games as an 18-year-old but Spurs were relegated. Hoddle truly bedded himself into the first team during Spurs' time in Division Two as the team were immediately promoted back to the First Division. In 1979 Hoddle made his England debut, but his international career was one of great frustration. At club level his quality was indisputable.

As is often the case with players who possess an abundance of skill and ability, Hoddle often made football look easy. His playing style was filled with elegance and grace in combination with being able to take the breath away with a sublime touch, pass, dribble or shot.

In 1983/84 Johan Cruyff decided to sign for Feyenoord for one final season. This shocked Dutch football as the Ajax legend had signed for their great rivals. Cruyff's presence helped to turn Feyenoord into domestic champions and that season gave him one more run in the UEFA Cup. There Feyenoord and Cruyff faced Spurs and Hoddle.

Cruyff is famous for his sharp footballing mind, strong opinions and uncanny knack for assessing exactly what is needed. The first-half performance of Tottenham versus Feyenoord was dazzling and it was led by Hoddle. His pinpoint, line-breaking, defence-splitting passes opened Feyenoord up over and over again.

'I wanted to test myself against the young star of the present,' said Cruyff. 'Glenn was a great player in my book. He played football the way that I wanted to see it played.'

Such praise from well-respected contemporaries and managers was not unusual.

'If Hoddle had been French he would have won well over 100 caps and the team would have been built around him,' said Michel Platini. Whatever one might think of Platini the administrator, he was a contemporary of Hoddle. His career coincided with Hoddle's and the French team was indeed built around Platini. Was Platini, a multi-time Ballon d'Or winner, in essence saying Hoddle was better than him?

Hoddle spent over a decade at Tottenham, playing almost 500 games and scoring over 100 goals. His time at the club earned many admirers but relatively few trophies. The UEFA Cup and two FA Cup wins were the fruits of his labours. In 1987 Hoddle decided to move to French football with Monaco. The manager, Arsène Wenger, built the team around Hoddle. Monaco would finish the season as champions of France. Using a diamond midfield, Hoddle was deployed as the attacking midfielder behind two strikers, Mark Hateley and George Weah. Hoddle's role was to dictate the play, create opportunities and seek out goalscoring chances for himself.

During the championship season Hoddle scored eight goals. The following season he netted 18 times in the league and twice in the European Cup, where Monaco were beaten in the quarter-finals by Galatasaray. Injuries meant Hoddle only played a handful of games in the two following seasons at Monaco before his surprising return to English football as player-manager of Swindon Town. After helping Swindon to promotion Hoddle spent two seasons as player-manager of Chelsea, with a third season in a manager-only capacity before becoming England manager.

Why didn't Hoddle play more for England?

English football spent decades valuing conservatism, industriousness, and the bulldog spirit. Players of the profile of Terry Butcher, willing to put his head through a defensive wall and bleed for his country, were held in higher esteem than players with the grace and elan of Glenn Hoddle. It is important to understand this, otherwise it is utterly inconceivable that England did not make better use of Hoddle. Even once we digest the emphasis on work rate, durability and grit, it remains extraordinary that England did not recognise what they had.

Or perhaps they did and they simply did not know how best to use it? Ron Greenwood and Sir Bobby Robson were the managers during Hoddle's international career. Both Greenwood and Robson used a 4-4-2 formation. Greenwood did use a playmaker, a role that Hoddle would have fitted well, but his choice was Trevor Brooking, perhaps influenced by Greenwood's West Ham ties. Robson appeared to trust Hoddle a little more than Greenwood but struggled to utilise him within his favoured 4-4-2 system. Robson eventually showed that he was willing to break the mould, first by switching the 'big man' in England's front pairing to a small, tricky, creative player, bringing in Peter Beardsley during the 1986 World Cup. Later, in 1990, he used a three-man defence, but by then it was too late for Hoddle. The Bobby Robson who had garnered European coaching experience in Portugal, the Netherlands and Spain might have been able to use Glenn Hoddle far better than the Bobby Robson of the 1980s.

England had a proliferation of high-quality central midfielders throughout the 1980s. The 1982 World Cup squad featured Hoddle, Brooking, Terry McDermott, Graham Rix, Bryan Robson and Ray Wilkins. In 1986 the central midfielders were Hoddle, Robson, Wilkins and Peter Reid. Across the squads there are three constants and these three were the outstanding players. Three into two does not go, an issue not dealt with by England until the late 2000s. Four defenders, two strikers and two wide players, this is the England way.

Yet it did not have to be.

Hoddle's final season at Spurs before heading to France was David Pleat's only season managing the club. Pleat found himself with a squad abundant with midfield talent. So he did the sensible thing and played them. Pleat dispensed with conventional English football wisdom and adopted a 4-5-1 formation. A creative hub of Hoddle, Ossie Ardiles and Chris Waddle (from the wing) supplied the ammunition to Clive Allen, which he hungrily accepted on his way to a 49-goal season. Hoddle was the creative heart of the team, free to do as he pleased, his talent unleashed to pick defences apart.

The best midfields need the right blend of players. We have established the characteristics of Glenn Hoddle but what of his colleagues in the England team? If England adopted a 4-5-1 who would have been in those spots? Hoddle plays as part of three-man central midfield alongside Ray Wilkins and Bryan Robson. Wilkins was well known for his stylish passing game, though sometimes criticised for passing sideways rather than forward, which might also have been seen as simply keeping possession. (Coincidentally, both Hoddle and Wilkins grew up in the same part of Greater London at the same time.) Bryan Robson was a dynamic, powerful, energetic and technically gifted central midfielder with an eye for goal. Robson scored 26 times in 90 games for England. Two similar central midfielders from more recent history, Steven Gerrard and Frank Lampard, scored 21 goals and 29 goals respectively in well over 100 appearances each. Robson's ratio outstripped both of them. The dynamic of Wilkins sitting deep and retaining possession, Robson working as a box-to-box midfielder and Hoddle playing in a more advanced playmaking role would appear to be one that is well balanced. A three-man midfield would also have helped to deal with a common problem experienced by England teams of that era against strong opposition, being outnumbered in midfield.

Hoddle and Wilkins would have been able to dictate the tempo from the centre and utilise their passing range to find the two wide players, John Barnes and Chris Waddle, both capable of playing on either wing, both capable of tucking inside and both capable of dominating opposition defences. Barnes and Waddle were also players who had some fantastic moments while wearing an England shirt but were often overlooked in favour of less creative but hard-working players.

All five of these players would be supplying the ammunition for Gary Lineker. Lineker was a missed penalty away from becoming England's record goalscorer. His strike rate of 48 goals in 80 appearances is inferior to only Jimmy Greaves and Harry Kane amongst players with over 40 England goals.

This line-up would have excited England fans around the country and struck fear into their opponents. Whoever England faced would not be able to switch off for a moment with the threats coming from all angles – a mixture of precision passing, dazzling dribbling and sharp shooting.

Not only would the line-up have been high in quality, but it would have been high in intelligence. Lineker was a speedy striker but not a particularly powerful one. His movement to find gaps was as key to his scoring ability as his pace. Barnes and Waddle were both intelligent enough that when their pace and running power declined they were able to play in central midfield playmaking roles. Wilkins and Robson showed their intelligence and game understanding not just in the way they performed but also in their post-playing careers as coaches and managers.

Then there was Hoddle, the most intelligent of them all, at least on the pitch. Technical ability is just one part of the equation. In terms of deftness of touch, arrow-like ball striking, smooth dribbling and passing that could split an atom, Hoddle was the equal of any player in world football. Hoddle could only execute these skills with such success because he could perceive his environment, seeing the pictures around him, always aware of his surroundings. Hoddle's brain was as brilliant as his feet.

If England had made these changes they would have impacted three World Cups where England did rather well, 1982, 1986 and 1990, and a Euros that England failed to qualify for in 1984 and a Euros they failed to have any impact in (1988).

At the 1982 World Cup England were undefeated. The format was complex, with twin group stages. England made a blistering start by beating a fantastic France side 3-1 in their opening game, Bryan Robson scoring in what was a then record 27 seconds. Robson would score again and then Paul Mariner added gloss to the scoreline. England used an asymmetric 4-4-2 midfield with Bryan Robson, Ray Wilkins and Graham Rix tucked in on one wing and Steve Coppell wide on the opposite side. Trevor Francis and Mariner were the strikers, with Hoddle spending the entire game on the bench. England won 3-1, so Hoddle's absence against a very strong France seems justified. The same line-up defeated Czechoslovakia 2-0, with Hoddle coming off the bench at half-time for an injured Robson. In the final group game Hoddle took Robson's place in the starting line-up and England won 1-0 against Kuwait.

This 100 per cent record qualified England for the three-team mini-group, the winner going into the semi-final. Their opponents were the World Cup hosts, Spain, and West Germany. Against West Germany Robson was restored to the starting line-up. Hoddle sat out the game as England created very little in a dull 0-0 draw consisting of mostly long shots and cleared crosses. In the final game England knew that they could reach the semi-final with a win. England used Trevor Francis and Graham Rix wide in a system closer to 4-2-4. With 25 minutes remaining they called upon Trevor Brooking and Kevin Keegan from the bench (both had been struggling with injury). They created one opportunity for Brooking, which he headed wide. When England were looking to create, they left their most creative player in his seat.

England only took one real wide player in their 1982 squad, Steve Coppell, but they could have deployed Francis wide in a 4-5-1, leaving the Hoddle, Wilkins and Robson axis in the centre. Mariner plays as the lone striker, but there is no doubt that the injury to Keegan, only three years removed from his Ballon d'Or win, was a significant blow to England. Switching Keegan in for Mariner makes the line-up significantly stronger.

In the first group stage little difference is made to the outcome. In the second group stage, in two extremely tight games, that extra spark of creativity could have made all the difference. It is not too big a stretch to suggest that one moment of Hoddle inspiration in both games sees England into the semi-final against France. One defence-splitting pass feeding in a galloping Coppell. One pinpoint pass releasing Francis to square to an onrushing Robson, two moments would be all that England required.

Germany and France played out a 3-3 epic, one of the great games in World Cup history. A successful England robs history of this epic encounter, but from an English perspective, they would rather have the success. Would England have beaten France or would France have gained revenge for that opening game defeat? It is quite likely that England are victorious and face a Paolo Rossi-inspired

Italy in the final. Once in the final anything could happen but Italy had seen off the extraordinary Brazil side of 1982, holding off the firepower of Zico, Socrates, Falcão and Eder, keeping them down to two goals while Rossi poached a hat-trick. If Italy were able to defeat that Brazil team it is likely that they defeat England. However, England with the added creativity of Hoddle reach the second World Cup Final in their history but can't quite get the win. (Another alternative is that Brazil beat Italy in the semi-final, and we have an epic England versus Brazil World Cup Final, which could have been the most incredible game.)

Qualification for the Euros was a tough school in the 1980s, especially as there were only eight spaces available at the tournament. England finished second in their five-team qualifying group behind Denmark. A surprise 1-0 loss at home to mid-80s Danish Dynamite ultimately proved costly. Even if England had qualified, a Platini-inspired France, playing in France, seemed to have victory written in their stars.

At the 1986 World Cup England started with a 1-0 defeat against Portugal. The team lined up with the Hoddle, Robson and Wilkins trio, but Hoddle played wide on the right with Waddle wide on the left. In their second game, against Morocco, the same line-up was deployed. However, Wilkins was sent off in the first half and the game finished 0-0. With Wilkins suspended and Bryan Robson now injured, manager Bobby Robson had to make changes. Hoddle remained in the team in a wide position, but Mark Hateley was removed from the front line in favour of a trickier, smaller, smarter player, Peter Beardsley. Beardsley dropping deeper into midfield from the forward line meant the England shape was now more akin to 4-5-1. England beat Poland 3-0 to progress, Gary Lineker's hat-trick setting him along the way to being top scorer at the tournament.

England used the same shape for the knockout stages, comfortably beating Paraguay 3-0 with Lineker scoring another two goals. The midfield line-up shifted significantly from the opening game to now feature Hoddle, Steve Hodge, Peter Reid and Trevor Steven. This midfield became extremely narrow, often looking more like Ron Greenwood's diamond. The density in the centre of the pitch was unable to prevent Diego Maradona scoring a magnificent solo goal and could do nothing about the infamous 'Hand of God' goal. The lack of width was eventually shown to have been a poor choice as once England were chasing the game from two goals behind they introduced John Barnes and Waddle on the wings. Barnes created a goal for Lineker along with multiple other opportunities.

Would the 4-5-1 have made a difference at the 1986 World Cup? England started with the key midfield players, though they were slightly out of position. Only in the final 20 minutes against Argentina did England have Waddle and Barnes on the pitch at the same time. Unlike in 1982 Hoddle played every game, but maybe not in a role or system that allowed him to flourish. Ultimately England's biggest hurdle to success at the 1986 World Cup was Argentina and Diego Maradona. Maradona is often cited as winning the 1986 tournament single-handed, with the two best teams of the tournament being Brazil and France, who clashed in a quarter-final before France were beaten by Germany in an epic semi-final for the second tournament in a row. Argentina were not the best team at the tournament but they possessed the best individual.

England's performances at Euro 88 were infamously poor. England lost all three of their group games, starting with a 1-0 defeat against the Republic of Ireland. The formation was a 4-4-2, with Neil Webb as the midfield playmaker alongside Robson. Waddle and Barnes started as the wingers with Beardsley alongside Lineker. Hoddle came on for Webb after an hour with England chasing the game. In the next match, against the Netherlands, Hoddle started alongside Robson with Webb dropping out. Waddle also dropped out of the team in favour of Trevor Steven. A Marco van Basten hat-trick nullified England's single Robson strike. After two games England were eliminated, leaving them to play out a dead rubber against the Soviet Union.

It might be viewed that England were unfortunate to face the two eventual finalists in their group, but the truth is that their performances on the pitch were very poor. Wilkins had struggled in 1988 with injury and form and missed the squad, but his place in our 4-5-1 could have been filled by Steve McMahon, who had just had a sensational season in the Beardsley, Barnes and Aldridge-inspired Liverpool side. The key to the group stage was the opening game against the Republic of Ireland. A more controlled and more creative performance could easily have won that game 1-0 rather than losing it 1-0. If that happens the defeat against the Dutch (should it have still happened, England and the Netherlands have a history of playing out draws) leaves England needing to win their final game against the Soviet Union. It also means that the Dutch have to win their final game having lost to the Soviet Union. If England win that game the Netherlands, England and the Soviet Union all end on the same number of points. In 1988 the Soviet Union progressed as group winners with the Netherlands in second. With all three teams level, it is quite possible that the Netherlands are the unfortunate team who are eliminated. England are then at least Euro 88 semi-finalists. Should they have taken the runners-up spot in the group their opponents would have been West Germany. Would England have won? It might be too big a stretch to imagine that England defeat West Germany and then go on to defeat the Soviet Union in the final. It is quite possible that in knocking the Dutch out of the tournament England hand the trophy to West Germany.

Thus far, by building the team around Hoddle we have seen England improve to semi-finalists at the 1982

World Cup, remain as quarter-finalists at the 1986 World Cup and reach the semi-finals of the 1988 European Championship.

Now comes the big one. Italia 90.

We have to start with two points regarding Hoddle here. He had just had two magnificent seasons with Monaco but he was injured for all of 1990. We therefore have to imagine not only that England built their team around Hoddle, but also that Hoddle was not injured and had carried on his sensational Monaco form.

The story of England at the 1990 World Cup is well documented. After two 0-0 draws Bobby Robson changed the team shape to a back five with a sweeper. England than edged past Egypt 1-0 to top the group, saw David Platt volley in a dramatic late extra-time winner against Belgium, beat Cameroon in the quarter-final thanks to a pair of Lineker penalties and then tearfully lose to West Germany in a shoot-out. The tournament saw Paul Gascoigne and David Platt break out as global stars, securing moves to Serie A, as Italy felt like the centre of the football world.

Less well documented is how turgid and defensive the tournament was as a whole. The West Germans were by far the best team of a tournament littered with fouls, timewasting and ill temper. Italia 90 was a launch pad for a number of law changes that speeded up football, creating a more entertaining spectacle.

Building the 1990 team around Hoddle is more challenging and impacts more players than in previous builds. This time it impacts the defence as much as the midfield and attack.

Robson and Wilkins were both 33 years old by the 1990 World Cup. Hoddle was 32. Bryan Robson remained in the starting XI due to his influence as captain, but injuries had caught up with him. Wilkins' form and fitness meant that his England days were behind him. The line-up needs to reflect that new players are coming through while still retaining Hoddle as the fulcrum.

England opened the tournament with a 4-4-2.

For their second game against the Netherlands the shape had become a 5-4-1.

By the West Germany semi-final the shape and personnel had changed even further into a 5-3-2.

In supposing that Hoddle is the heart of this team the shape needs to revert to 4-5-1. Mark Wright is not brought into the team as sweeper. Robson is removed from the line-up, as is Peter Beardsley. Steve McMahon comes into the midfield but likely is eventually usurped by David Platt.

When Platt comes into the side the midfield triangle flattens out a little with Hoddle's playmaking abilities dropping a little deeper to enable Platt's off-the-ball running and Gascoigne's dribbling on the ball.

England top their group in either version of events, perhaps with two wins with Hoddle in the side, rather than just the one snatched against Egypt. Removing Mark Wright from the team removes the scorer of the winning goal against Egypt, but this more creative line-up scores from open play rather than relying on a late set piece. It is the same story against Belgium, with England scoring during the 90 minutes and not waiting for a late David Platt goal. This removes one of the classic goals of England history and David Platt's breakout moment, but instead it allows Barnes and Waddle to make their mark as Hoddle's raking passes set them free.

The thriller against Cameroon remains the same, a more exciting England line-up possibly adding a fourth goal for additional shine, but England win through. Once again the big one is the West Germany game. England and Germany both played with five-man defences, though Germany were closer to 3-5-2 than 5-3-2. Their width came from Andreas Brehme and Thomas Berthold. The three-man midfields directly matched up. With England now using a 4-5-1 they are able to create overloads in wide areas, especially with John Barnes and the persistent, stamina-sapping overlaps of Stuart Pearce. England were very close to winning the game in the original version of the tournament, but here Hoddle feeds Barnes with an exquisite switch of play, Barnes squares up his wing-back, teasing him in with stepovers until Pearce gallops past on the overlap. Barnes slides the pass, enabling Pearce to flash a ball across the box. Lineker poaches, steering a shot past Bodo Illgner and England are into the final against Argentina.

Argentina and Maradona were not the same team as at the 1986 World Cup. They smuggled their way into the final with toughness and willpower. The final in 1990 was a foul-filled affair, with Argentina eventually having two players sent off. Germany won a dire game with a late Andreas Brehme penalty. Now England survive the scrap. Argentina concede a late penalty. Lineker steps up and calmly strokes England to a 1-0 win and their second World Cup victory.

Glenn Hoddle, with impeccable timing, retires from international football the day after winning the trophy. He retires with England having built their team around him, well over 100 caps and a World Cup winners' medal.

WHAT IF THESE CRAZY TRANSFERS HAD ACTUALLY HAPPENED?

Maradona signs for Sheffield United

In 1978 Sheffield United signed River Plate midfielder Alex Sabella. Around the same time Ossie Ardiles and Ricky Villa joined Spurs, sparking the first wave of exotic imports into English football. Sheffield United's scouting trip did not initially identify Sabella as their transfer target. It was a 17-year-old Diego Maradona. A deal was set up, but Sheffield United pulled out over the fee, supposedly around £200,000.

Sheffield United were a Second Division (Championship) team in the pre-Premier League era. They had been relegated two seasons earlier and had ambitions to return. Would a young Maradona have been enough to get them promoted? Maybe not immediately, but certainly within a few seasons. Undoubtedly Maradona would have been targeted and had lumps kicked out of him. Diego fell out of love with Barcelona before joining Napoli, but perhaps he falls in love with Sheffield and England. Perhaps after inspiring Sheffield United a big fee unites him with his compatriots at Spurs. Perhaps by 1986 Maradona is still playing in England when he punches the ball past Shilton.

Imagine the reception he would receive on the opening day of the 1986/87 season.

Rivaldo signs for Bolton

In the early 2000s Bolton Wanderers had created their very own stable of mini-galacticos. Sam Allardyce's reputation for playing direct football did not put off a group of talented entertainers who signed for the club. Youri Djorkaeff, Jay-Jay Okocha, Iván Campo and Fernando Hierro all enjoyed time at the then Reebok Stadium. When Rivaldo's contract was ended at AC Milan he very nearly joined the Bolton ranks. According to legend, Rivaldo's agents met with Bolton in Manchester but he chose to play in Greece instead.

Bolton could have been globetrotteresque with great entertainers up front playing off Kevin Davies, holding the ball up and bringing others into play, Bolton using a form of 4-2-3-1. Bolton finished an excellent eighth in 2003/04 but with superstar Rivaldo in the ranks they could be challenging for fourth place and buzzing around the Champions League.

Sam Allardyce for England.

Radamel Falcao and Edinson Cavani sign for Aston Villa

The presence of a compatriot often appears to lend credence to a transfer. Between 2001 and 2007 the Colombian striker Juan Pablo Ángel made over 200 appearances for Aston Villa. Fellow Colombian Falcao was also at Ángel's former club River Plate, making the path even more legitimate. Once one South American striker is in the works another is easy to believe. Cavani was at Palermo in Italy, on the verge of superstar status.

Cavani and Falcao would both play for Manchester United at different times towards the ends of their careers but prior to that they forged reputations as prolific top-level European goalscorers. Aston Villa were managed by Martin O'Neill in the mid-2000s and consistently challenged for fifth and sixth place. Could the extra firepower of these two goal machines have pushed Villa into the Champions League places or even higher?

Robert Lewandowski signs for Blackburn

Another Sam Allardyce and Lancashire story. Allardyce had a few solid seasons with Blackburn Rovers at the end of the 2000s. In the 2009/10 season goals were hard to come by as no Blackburn player reached double figures in the league. The search for a striker began. Robert Lewandowski had scored 21 goals in 31 games for Lech Poznań. Then a volcanic ash cloud and Borussia Dortmund intervened.

Lewandowski wasn't a smash in his first Dortmund season, scoring just eight league goals, but in his second campaign he netted 22 times and became one of the most prolific and consistent scorers in European football. Blackburn would finish 15th in 2010/11. Relegation would swiftly follow. How would Lewandowski have performed in England? Given the physical and technical similarities between the Bundesliga and the Premier League his performance would likely be very similar. Blackburn would have been safe for a number of seasons before an inevitable windfall when the big clubs would come calling.

Zlatan Ibrahimovic signs for Arsenal

Even at 16 years old Zlatan had extraordinary confidence. Arsenal had spotted him while still playing for Malmo. Arsène Wenger invited him to training. Infamously, Zlatan refused and signed for Ajax.

Had Zlatan signed for Arsenal at that stage he would have been joining the club at a time when they were double winners. Dennis Bergkamp was pulling the strings, Ian Wright was coming towards the end of his time with the Gunners but Nicolas Anelka was emerging. Wenger was happy to play youngsters, so Zlatan would likely break into the team once Anelka left, playing in tandem with Bergkamp. Bergkamp and Zlatan would have been an exciting and successful partnership. Perhaps so successful that there is no need to sign Thierry Henry.

Zidane signs for Blackburn

Blackburn were Premier League champions in 1994/95. Despite losing in the final minute against Liverpool at Anfield the team managed by Kenny Dalglish and funded by the spending power of Jack Walker topped the table. Captain Tim Sherwood held the trophy aloft.

Dalglish wanted to strengthen his squad and a deal was done to sign a 23-year-old from Bordeaux. The deal was all but completed until Jack Walker uttered the infamous words: 'Why would we want to sign Zidane when we have Tim Sherwood?'

With that the prospect of seeing Zidane linking with Alan Shearer went up in smoke. Rather than seeing the two powerhouses together, devastating the Premier League, Shearer signed for Newcastle and Blackburn went into decline. Had Shearer and Zidane been together for half a decade Shearer might have reached 300 Premier League goals – perhaps Blackburn might even have won the Champions League.

John Barnes signs for AC Milan

In Italy there is a popular myth that the signing of Luther Blissett from Watford was a huge admin error. In the early to mid-80s there was a raft of British players signing for Italian clubs. The most mystifying was AC Milan paying £1 million for Watford striker Blissett. Blissett had scored 27 top-flight goals the season before he signed for Milan but only scored five in Serie A.

111

The story endured that Milan had not made a mistake in judging the quality of the player, just that they had signed the wrong man.

Barnes' rampaging wing play might not have been best suited to Serie A at the time but the pressure to score would not have been there. Barnes would have been a creative success, exciting the fans. At the time Serie A rules meant that only three foreign players could be in the starting line-up. This would pose problems for the evolution of Milan. With Barnes a success and fans' favourite, which of Marco van Basten, Ruud Gullit and Frank Rijkaard would miss out?

Ronaldinho signs for Manchester United

In the summer of 2003 Manchester United thought they had their man. Joining from PSG, Ronaldinho. United had sold Beckham to Real Madrid, with Barcelona trying hard but failing to capture Beckham. Barcelona broke the bank (they had help from Catalonia and Nike) to take Ronaldinho away from Manchester United.

The idea of Manchester United signing a great player is in no way absurd, but the knock-on effect of Ronaldinho at Manchester United is immense. Firstly, you would have a three Ronnies attacking line-up – Ronaldinho, Ronaldo and Rooney. The entertainment value from that trio would have been amazing. At Barcelona they lose the player who would be their talisman until the emergence of Messi. They would likely miss out on two league titles and a Champions League without him. Xavi and Iniesta are emerging at the time, as well as Fàbregas. Fàbregas left for Arsenal – with a lack of success, might Barcelona have sold on other young talents to fund big-name deals? Fàbregas. Xavi. Iniesta. Messi.

Iniesta signs for Rangers

During the early 2000s Glasgow Rangers were in an extremely successful period. Laden with trophies and boasting players of the quality of Ronald de Boer and Mikel Arteta, they were able to compete on the European stage.

Clever transfer deals were a part of this success. Signing a young Arteta was an example of this. Arteta could not break into the Barcelona team. He went on loan to PSG. Rangers were impressed with his performances there and paid £6 million before Arteta had even made a Barcelona appearance.

Rangers and Barcelona attempted to get Iniesta to Rangers as a loan deal, but this collapsed. What if Rangers had offered Barcelona £6 million and secured his services? Rangers would have added one of the great midfielders of his generation to their side. Rangers would also have secured more domestic titles and had a tilt at European glory with a player who all of Europe would have coveted. Only a huge fee would have taken Iniesta from Rangers, money that might have prevented the dark financial collapse that Rangers suffered.

Denis Law signs for Liverpool

Manchester United legend Denis Law famously had not one, but two spells at their local rivals Manchester City. United fans are quite forgiving of this, despite the 'legendary' goal that relegated United in 1974 when the two faced each other on the final day (results meant United were down and the goal made no difference).

Law might never have played for either club. He signed for Manchester City from Second Division Huddersfield in 1959. The same year the Huddersfield manager left and wanted to take Law, his star player, with him. Bill Shankly wanted Denis Law to go with him to Liverpool. The deal never happened, and Liverpool signed Ian St John to partner Roger Hunt. Had it gone through, the United holy trinity of Best, Law and Charlton would never have been and Busby might never have found that out-and-out striker his team needed. Meanwhile, Liverpool would have two of the most prolific strikers of the 1960s together.

WHAT IF THE CHAMPIONS LEAGUE WAS STILL FOR CHAMPIONS ONLY?

It's a lie.

The early 1990s was a time of rebranding. The First Division became the Premier League. The European Cup became the Champions League. Which is what it was, a league for the champions of all of the leagues of Europe. At its inauguration in 1992 the Champions League was telling the truth.

It didn't take long for the lies to begin. In 1997 the competition became the Champions and Runners-Up League. The old European Cup name would have been far more apt.

For over 20 years the European Cup had pitted the teams at the peak of their powers against one another. The UEFA Cup swept up the best of the rest and it was often considered that due to the depth of quality involved the UEFA Cup was the harder tournament to win. Less glamorous, but more difficult. This meant that there were multiple league championship and UEFA Cup doubles as the teams involved were often on the rise.

The phenomenon of two teams from the same nation facing each other in the European Cup was only possible if the holders of the competition failed to win their domestic league. Just this happened in 1978/79 when Liverpool faced Nottingham Forest. Liverpool were the reigning European champions, with Forest the English champions. Forest won through and took Liverpool's European crown as well as their domestic title.

These rare events became more commonplace once the Champions League expanded even further. The parameters shifted from winners and runners-up to include third- and fourth-placed teams. UEFA were desperately fighting off a European Super League by making it very difficult for the powerhouses of European football to fail to qualify for the big show. The rewards for a smaller team having an unexpectedly good season are now greater than a UEFA Cup place, but do they really have a chance of winning the Champions League? How many times has the trophy been won by domestic league winners rather than teams who had finished in second, third and fourth place the previous season?

Since the Champions League became less exclusive and allowed non-champions to enter, only one team outside of the big four leagues has won the competition. That was José Mourinho's Porto in 2004. Up to and including the 2021 final (won by Chelsea) the tournament has been won by ten teams who earned their place as league champions, eight teams who earned their spot as league runners-up, two teams who finished third and four teams who had finished fourth. Though the champion position has yielded the most winners, there have been more non-champion winners of the competition, more winners who would not have been eligible under the original rules.

Under a champions-only system a number of famous footballing events would not have been able to take place. When Manchester United won their famous 1999 treble their qualification for the Champions League came by virtue of finishing runners-up to Arsenal in the 1997/98 season. Chelsea are two-time Champions League winners, their first coming after finishing in second place, their second victory after finishing in fourth position. AC Milan have won two tournaments since the opening up of qualification rules, but neither as Serie A champions. The great Messi and Barcelona side of 2008/09 won the Champions League having finished third the previous season. Both of Liverpool's Champions League triumphs followed fourth-place finishes. If the old qualification rules had remained in place Liverpool would have gone from 1985 until 2020 without playing a single Champions League game.

By allowing clubs to qualify through top-four finishes some of the essence of European football's elite competition has been eroded.

For me there are five trophies. The first is to win the Premier League, the second is to win

the Champions League, the third is to qualify
for the Champions League, the fourth is to win
the FA Cup, the fifth is to win the League Cup.

Arsène Wenger

With that 2012 quote the die was well and truly cast.
For many that way of thinking had long existed but few
dared to air such a sentiment to the British public. Wenger
was vilified by some – third place quite simply is not a
trophy – but it has become evident just how important
Champions League qualification has become.

The incentive shifted. Once first place was everything
and if you had not finished first you were building
towards it. Now the top four was everything. Booking
your ticket to the show was vital, initially because the
Champions League money was a huge financial incentive
(it still is, though perhaps not to the degree it once was)
and then because it became established as the ultimate
level of football. The absolute pinnacle. Beyond any
international tournament. The true stars, the footballing
gods, performed on the Champions League stage. In order
to attract the stars to your team you needed to book your
big ticket. The FA Cup did not book your ticket. The
League Cup did not book your big ticket. Top four was
the only way.

Had the Champions League remained only for
champions the FA Cup might have maintained its lustre.
Almost certainly the Cup Winners' Cup would not have

been extinguished and merged into the UEFA Europa competitions, remaining an exclusive trophy and one of the more difficult to add to the collection. The FA Cup has become the domain of the top teams with fewer surprise winners, this despite the teams with 'bigger fish to fry' rotating their squads heavily for the competition. What prohibits the shock winners is that now the lesser lights rotate their squads themselves, sacrificing a chance to win the cup in favour of keeping players fit to secure another three points in their league-related struggles. Such has been the fate of the FA Cup.

Had a champions-only format remained, the hierarchy of European football may have a very different look to it. With less competition depth and fewer opportunities for the established elite some different names might have appeared on the trophy. Or some clubs might have more competition wins to their name.

In the period after allowing entry to non-champions, Manchester United won the competition twice, including their famous victory in 1999 as a non-champion entrant. However, during this time they were English champions nine times. In a more slimlined Champions League would they have had a greater chance of success than in a tournament packed with big-name teams? Allowing the glamour names to qualify more easily has increased the marketability of the Champions League and helped line their pockets, but has it actually made the trophy harder for them to win? Just as it was once harder to win the UEFA Cup due to the depth of quality. Until Real Madrid won three trophies in a row under Zinedine Zidane no club had successfully defended the Champions League, largely down to that depth of quality. Under a champions-only rule the depth decreases significantly. The Manchester United teams that won nine Premier League titles would have possessed sufficient calibre to have potentially won more Champions League trophies. Indeed, they were the victims of Barcelona in Rome in 2008/09, a tournament they had qualified for as champions, while Barcelona had finished third in La Liga. The 1999/2000 final was won by non-league champions Real Madrid. The 2010/11 tournament was won by non-champions Chelsea.

The squads of Manchester United in the early 2000s with Beckham, Scholes, Keane, Giggs, Cole, Yorke, Sheringham et al would have seriously challenged for a few titles. As would the United squads from 2006–11 which won four out of five Premier League titles with Ferdinand, Rooney, Ronaldo, Scholes, Tevez, Vidić and more. Might Manchester United have won four Champions League trophies rather than two, mimicking the success of Liverpool in the late 70s and early 80s?

There have been many surprising winners of domestic leagues denied their opportunity to shock Europe in the manner of Nottingham Forest. Forest won the First Division from nowhere and then won back-to-back European Cups in 1979 and 1980, benefitting from a smaller field. Their two finals were against Malmo and Hamburg, not the glamorous powerhouses of European aristocracy. In 1978/79 Forest undoubtedly benefitted from a path to the final made up of AEK Athens, Grasshoppers and Cologne. Their biggest task was in the first round against Liverpool.

In English football there have been few surprise league winners, Leicester being the exception. In Italy only Lazio and Roma have broken the Juventus, Inter and AC Milan stranglehold. Nonetheless, one of those two teams could have had a better chance to join the Champions League roll of honour in a field of fewer runners. In Spain Atletico Madrid (twice), Deportivo La Coruna and Valencia (twice) were able to break through the vice-like grip of Barcelona and Real Madrid. Though Valencia did reach two Champions League finals, neither was after qualifying as league title winners. Atletico reached a final, but not after qualifying as domestic champions.

Until relatively recently the Bundesliga had a good spread of teams winning the domestic league. Between 2000 and 2012 the league was won by Bayern Munich (five times), Borussia Dortmund (three), Werder Bremen, VfB Stuttgart and Wolfsburg. Sadly for Bremen, Stuttgart and Wolfsburg the European elite prevented them from making any real impact on the Champions League.

One team from outside of the European elite arguably suffered far more than anyone else because of the decision to allow non-champions to enter the Champions League in the late 1990s. No team from Eastern Europe has won the big competition since Red Star Belgrade in 1991. One team possibly should have and came extremely close. Valeriy Lobanovskyi had a legendary managerial career, managing Dynamo Kyiv three times, first from 1973–82, then 1984–90 and finally 1997–2002. In that final reign his Kyiv team came extremely close to winning the Champions League trophy.

During the 1997/98 Champions League season the Kyiv strike partnership of Serhiy Rebrov and Andriy Shevchenko caught the eye. Rebrov netted eight Champions League goals, while Shevchenko notched six. In the group stage Kyiv faced Barcelona and brushed them aside 3-0 in the home game. At the Nou Camp came an even more spectacular result. Lobanovskyi utilised pressing and counter-attacking tactics to rip Barcelona apart. Shevchenko blitzed a first half hat-trick and Rebrov rounded off the scoring with a late goal, a 4-0 win at the home of the mighty *Blaugrana*. Juventus would knock them out in the quarter-finals, but Lobanovskyi, Rebrov and Shevchenko were just getting warmed up.

The very next season Shevchenko scored ten Champions League goals, while Rebrov scored another eight. They cruised through the group stage into the quarter-finals. There they faced Real Madrid. The first leg at the Bernabeu finished 1-1. In Kyiv the second leg finished 2-0 with a Shevchenko double. On to the semi-final with Bayern Munich. At half-time Kyiv led 2-0, Shevchenko with another double. Kyiv's high-tempo, team-first football seemed to have them on the brink of the Champions League Final. Michael Tarnat scored moments after half-time but Kyiv scored a third to restore their two-goal cushion. With 12 minutes remaining things started to go wrong. Stefan Effenberg made it 3-2 and then Carsten Jancker equalised with two minutes remaining. The lead evaporated. In the second leg Bayern won 1-0 to set up their infamous final with Manchester United.

Tremendous, captivating performances from Dynamo. Many teams have seen enthralling campaigns dramatically ended, but why is this significant? In our context of discussing a champions-only Champions League it is worth pointing out that Bayern Munich had qualified as runners-up in the Bundesliga, and would then go on to lose the final to the Premier League runners-up. In a champions-only competition these two hurdles are no longer in the way of Kyiv and Lobanovskyi adds the Champions League to his legend.

The seeding for the tournament in 1998/99 put the defending champions (Real Madrid) plus seven national champions straight into the group stage. The runners-up went into the second qualifying round but other champions had to start in the first qualifying round. Kyiv themselves began at that stage.

The line-up of actual champions for the 1998/99 Champions League was:

Moments That Could Have Changed Football Forever

Dynamo Kiev	Kaiserslautern	Lens	Arsenal
Juventus	Barcelona	Ajax	Porto
Spartak Moscow	Sparta Prague	Croatia Zagreb	Rosenborg
Galatasaray	Olympiacos	Sturm Graz	Brondby
Grasshopper	Dinamo Tbilisi	Skonto	Cliftonville
Anorthosis	Litex Lovech	Valetta	LKS Lodz
Celtic	Sileks	Barry Town	Ujpest
Beitar Jerusalem	Kareda Siauliai	St Patrick's Athletic	Club Brugge
Maribor	Obilic	B36 Torshavn	Kosice
Dinamo Minsk	Zimbru Chisanau	Vllaznia	Steaua Bucuresti
IBV	Flora Tallinn	Jeunesse Esch	Halmstad
HJK	Yerevan	Kapaz	

In that field, stripped of European giants such as Inter, Bayern Munich, Manchester United and Benfica, the path for Kyiv would have looked far less difficult.

Undoubtedly Juventus and Barcelona are the standout teams. In the actual 1998/99 Champions League they were beaten in the semi-final by a Roy Keane-inspired Manchester United. Juventus made Manchester United scrap but their overall quality that season was a long way below par, finishing seventh in Serie A. This was despite a squad possessing such luminaries as Zinedine Zidane, Edgar Davids, Alessandro Del Piero and Didier Deschamps. High-quality players but not a fully functioning team. Barcelona finished their season as La Liga winners, but only finished third in their Champions League group stage, a group that contained Bayern Munich and Manchester United. In a champions-only competition they most likely make it beyond the group stage. In the Barcelona ranks were two Ballon d'Or winners, Luis Figo and Rivaldo. Yet they were not a dominant Barcelona team, champions with only 79 points and suffering seven La Liga losses. It was only a season earlier that Dynamo crushed Barcelona both home and away with largely the same line-up. Their chief tormentors, Rebrov and Shevchenko, remained in place to strike fear into their defence again, running into the large, open Nou Camp spaces.

Arsenal were in a period in which they struggled to escape the group stages of the Champions League. Arsenal and Kyiv faced each other in the 1998/99 group stage and were unable to gain a victory, Kyiv winning 3-1 in Ukraine and drawing 1-1 at Wembley. Ajax would finish the Eredivisie season as the sixth-best team and unable to emerge from their Champions League group against Porto, Croatia Zagreb and Olympiacos. Not a vintage Ajax team. The legendary pair of strikers would seem more than capable of eliminating the Dutch side.

What impact might that have had on Dynamo Kyiv, being the champions of Europe at the close of the century? Might that have tempted Shevchenko and Rebrov to stay at the club? AC Milan's glamour might have been enough to claim Shevchenko but Rebrov would surely have been less attracted to Spurs. Kyiv might have been able to claim multiple European titles, in the manner of Ajax in the early 1970s, when their success came from seemingly nowhere. Kyiv's very own hat-trick of European titles.

WHAT IF ENGLISH CLUBS HAD NOT BEEN BANNED FROM EUROPE IN 1985?

On 29 May 1985 Liverpool met Juventus in the European Cup Final at the Heysel Stadium in Brussels. Before the game, violence erupted when Liverpool fans charged towards the Juventus section. Juventus fans trying to escape the mayhem were crushed, a stadium wall collapsed and 39 people, mainly Italians, were killed, with over 600 others injured. It seems unbelievable from this distance that the game went on to be played. Juventus won 1-0 through a Platini penalty. However, within days UEFA had banned English clubs from European competition indefinitely, although this did not extend to the England national team. The ban lasted until 1991, with Liverpool returning one year later. But what if the 1985 European Cup Final had passed without the violence and English clubs had not been banned from Europe? What effect did this have on the nation's game and the clubs that missed out on European competition?

Violence and hooliganism off the field had a big impact on English football. Between 1982 and 1992 the average attendance across all games in Division One, the top tier, fell below 22,000 for the first time in 50 years. On the field there was still the full-blooded, end-to-end excitement that makes the Premier League of today so marketable to a global audience. There was the emergence of a great rivalry between the two Merseyside clubs in the mid-80s as the Division One league title was swapped between them over four years. And in 1989, one of the most exciting finishes to a league season occurred, when Michael Thomas scored a last-minute winner at Anfield to give Arsenal the title over Liverpool on goals scored. On the field the drama was undoubtedly still there.

The England national team had mixed results under Bobby Robson, with an abject 1988 European Championship finals performance sandwiched in between creditable campaigns in the World Cups of 1986 and 1990. Yet without European club football, the English game inevitably turned inward. English clubs had enjoyed outstanding success in Europe in the run-up to Heysel, winning the European Cup seven years out of eight between 1977 and 1984. The passion, the glamour and the glory of those great nights had gone.

The European ban hit Liverpool Football Club very hard. They had won four European Cups between 1977 and 1984 and the competition, the exhilarating nights it produced at Anfield, and the fans' legendary stories of travelling, were now woven into the club's history. It is not unreasonable to suggest Liverpool would have added at least one more European Cup to their total. Steaua Bucharest, Porto and PSV all won the competition immediately after the ban. They were fine sides, playing exceptional football, but Liverpool's greater experience in the competition would surely have seen them through at least once. At the end of the decade they would have run into the great AC Milan team featuring the brilliant Dutch trio of Rijkaard, Gullit and Van Basten. But what a game that could have produced, as the Liverpool team transitioned from Rush and Dalglish to Barnes and Beardsley. It is also highly likely that Liverpool would have gone very close in the 1987 UEFA Cup, which was won by Bayer Leverkusen.

Liverpool were eventually allowed back into European competition in 1992. They would have to wait nine years for their next European trophy, the UEFA Cup in 2001, and 12 years for their next Champions League title in 2005. Momentum was lost. It took 30 years for the club to win its next top-tier title in the Premier League. The ban had ended Liverpool's period of domination both at home and abroad.

No club could have been more disappointed by the ban on English clubs than Everton. From 1970 to 1984 they had watched their rivals across Stanley Park rack up eight Division One titles and four European Cups. But in 1985, the tide had turned. Everton not only won the Division One title, they also won the European Cup Winners' Cup. Their superb side fought thrilling battles with Liverpool on the domestic front. Their time had come. They had experienced European success. Now it was *their* turn to bring home the European Cup. And who is to say they wouldn't? Gary Lineker arrived in 1986. Although Everton finished double runners-up to Liverpool at home, they would surely have gone close in the European Cup. That year the semi-finalists were Anderlecht, Gothenburg, Barcelona and eventual winners Steaua Bucharest. Everton would have been confident against any of these sides. The following year they wrestled the Division One title back from Liverpool. But with no European football, manager Howard Kendall left to manage Athletic Bilbao. Lineker had already departed for Barcelona. The prestige of a European Cup would have had an enormous impact, especially on the signings Everton would have made, and on the improvement of Goodison Park. The great side broke up. Decline set in. Since 1987, one of the giants of English football has added a solitary FA Cup win in 1995 to its trophy cabinet. The searing sense of frustration of 'what might have been' is still apparent today.

The ban impacted across so many English clubs. Every team that was successful in the late 80s and early 90s would have a 'what if' tale to tell. Arsenal won the thrilling league title in 1989 and would have come up against the AC Milan team at its height in the European Cup. But previous experience of competition at this level would surely have stood them in good stead in 1991/92 when they went out of the competition against Benfica after extra time. The large English contingent in the Arsenal team would also have benefitted, which could only have helped the national team.

Manchester United have a proud history in European competition, being the first English entrants into the European Cup, and eventually becoming the first winners, despite coming up against the disapproval of the FA at the time. In some ways it is fitting that they were the first English side to lift a trophy, the 1991 European Cup Winners' Cup, after the ban was lifted. By now Alex Ferguson was in charge. But Ron Atkinson might well have led his side to UEFA Cup glory, especially in 1987 when Gothenburg were the winners. And what if he had? Would the Fergie years have merely been postponed, or happened at all?

Spurs qualified for the UEFA Cup twice during this time. They were the first winners of the competition. In 1989/90 they finished third in Division One as Paul Gascoigne and Gary Lineker dovetailed in thrilling fashion. They would surely have broken into the all-Italian final of Juventus v Fiorentina.

There is a strong argument to suggest that the ban had its biggest impact on the clubs who were not regulars in European competition. What fun Oxford could have had in the UEFA Cup and Coventry in the European Cup Winners' Cup. Norwich qualified for the UEFA Cup three times during the ban. What a difference that could have made, and given their barnstorming games against

Bayern Munich in 1993, who is to say how far they could have gone? Forest, too, qualified twice for the UEFA Cup during this time and perhaps could have given Brian Clough another trophy to add to his two European Cups.

Even after the ban was lifted, English clubs missed out on qualifying for Europe through the reduction in the 'co-efficient'. It took until 1995/96 for England to regain its four places in the UEFA Cup. A whole host of clubs would have qualified, all of them missing out on revenue, potential signings and of course the chance of glory.

Yet out of all the 'what ifs' surrounding the effect of the ban on English clubs from Europe, there is one that is surely the most intriguing of all. In 1988 Wimbledon produced one of the greatest upsets in the history of FA Cup finals by defeating league champions Liverpool 1-0. They were dubbed the 'Crazy Gang'.

So, what if Vinny and Lawrie and Dennis and Fash had taken their place in the European Cup Winners' Cup of 1989?

The opening round sees Wimbledon drawn against Dutch team Roda. The first leg is at Plough Lane. The noise in the tight little ground is up another level, the dressing room is bouncing, the ghetto blaster is like an extra man. Roda try to play their football. They never stand a chance. The first long throw is flicked on by Fashanu and Wise bundles the ball over the line. Jones makes his presence felt with one crunching tackle after another. Fashanu outjumps the

Dutch defence from a corner and Wimbledon go in 2-0 up at half-time. It's more of the same in the second half, but Wise adds a third after a neat one-two with Sanchez. Terry Gibson rounds off the scoring to give the Dons a healthy first-leg lead.

In the second leg Jones is booked after just five minutes as the referee tries to give Roda some protection. Smeets pulls one back for the Dutch to give them some hope at half-time. But five minutes into the second half a free kick is launched into the Roda box and after a scramble Sanchez lashes home. Wimbledon go through to the second round 5-1 on aggregate.

In the second round the Dons are drawn against Sredets Sofia, with the first leg in Bulgaria. Sredets are more streetwise than Roda, technically efficient and have a real star leading the line. Hristo Stoichkov gives John Scales and Eric Young a torrid time and his two goals look to have put his side in command. With just two minutes to play, Wimbledon's keeper Sullivan launches the ball into the Sredets box, Fashanu nods down and Carlton Fairweather, on as a sub, scores a vital away goal.

The return leg is played on a typical November night, swirling wind, intermittent horizontal rain. The Bulgarians fight fire with fire and the tackling from both sides is 'fierce'. Stoichkov is finding it difficult in the conditions. Chances are few and far between. After an hour Fashanu bustles into the box. In a flurry of elbows and arms he finishes up on the floor. The referee points to the spot. The Sredets defenders are incensed. Fash picks himself up, and in driving rain, takes just two steps before side-footing the ball home. If the score stays at 1-0 the Crazy Gang will win the tie on away goals. Now it is Wimbledon who come under pressure. With time running out, Sredets throw everything at them. Rallied by captain Wise, their indomitable spirit takes them through.

Everyone is hoping for a dream tie against Barcelona in the quarter-finals. Could Johan Cruyff's side do it on a wet Wednesday at Plough Lane? Wimbledon are drawn to face Sampdoria, with the first leg in Italy. Vinny Jones is in the press telling everyone he will 'eat the eyeties for breakfast'.

The Crazy Gang arrive in Genoa in good spirits. The Italians, however, are more than ready. They have both steel and talent in their ranks. Above all, they are streetwise.

As Wimbledon launch the ball forward from the kick-off, captain and sweeper Luca Pellegrini goes down clutching his face after a challenge from Fashanu. Within five minutes Vinny Jones has been booked for a tackle on Salsano. Things get worse, as Gianluca Vialli opens the scoring with a terrific volley. As Wimbledon try to get a foothold in the game disaster arrives in the shape of a red card for Jones. Roberto Mancini draws him into a foul and does enough to convince the referee to produce a second yellow. Vialli adds a second from a clever corner routine. Wimbledon are in trouble. Two minutes into the second half Fashanu rattles the bar with a bullet header. It is the last act of defiance. Mancini adds a third for Sampdoria. Wimbledon lose their heads as the bookings tot up. Five minutes from the end, Dennis Wise is sent off for arguing. Mancini dribbles around Sullivan to add a fourth.

Manager Bobby Gould says his side will give everything in the second leg. And they do. Sampdoria attempt to take the sting out of the game. Their trainer is on the pitch constantly, the Wimbledon crowd now booing loudly at each Italian who goes down. Just before half-time Lawrie Sanchez gives the Dons a glimmer of hope as he scores off an inswinging corner from Alan Cork. After an hour Terry Phelan goes on a mazy run from left-back, squares into the Sampdoria box and Fashanu slides home. Could the miracle be on? Sadly not. With Wimbledon pressing forward, Vialli and Mancini exchange passes and Vialli kills the tie with a neat chip over Sullivan. Wimbledon bow out 2-5 on aggregate.

So what if Heysel had not happened? What if the English clubs had not been banned? One European Cup, two UEFA Cups and one Cup Winners' Cup is probably a conservative estimate of the trophies that would have been won. But with extra experience against top European opposition, would Walker and Waddle, would Gazza and Lineker have had that little extra big-match know-how? Would England have brought home the World Cup in 1990?

WHAT IF STEVEN GERRARD HAD SIGNED FOR CHELSEA?

'How can I think of leaving Liverpool after a night like this?'

It is 25 May 2005 and Liverpool have just completed an extraordinary comeback in Istanbul. From three goals behind at half-time they drew level, taking the game to penalties and triumphing to win the Champions League.

The Miracle of Istanbul.

It is all the more miraculous because this Liverpool team had endured a sub-standard season in all competitions apart from the Champions League. Manager Rafa Benítez was generally considered to have over-performed by reaching the final of the competition. The squad he inherited for his first season at Anfield was not chock-full of world-class players. Liverpool had a number of extremely good players, but were lacking quality in key positions. In a one-off game they could be hard to beat, but over the course of a full season their lack of depth showed, finishing fifth in the league while Chelsea romped to the title.

José Mourinho was also in his debut season in 2004/05. He had won the Champions League the previous season with Porto. Along with a new manager the Roman Abramovich oligarch era splashed the cash on Paulo Ferreira, Petr Čech, Arjen Robben, Didier Drogba and Ricardo Carvalho, players who would be key to the club's success for much of the next decade. These players arrived on top of a squad that already included John Terry, William Gallas, Claude Makélélé, Damien Duff and Joe Cole. Chelsea would finish the league season with 95 points and only 15 goals conceded.

The next season Chelsea added Lassana Diarra, Shaun Wright-Phillips and Michael Essien. They would be champions once more, claiming 91 points. Despite Chelsea's success, Mourinho was never fully satisfied with his central midfield.

The signings of Diarra and Essien are evidence of this in 2005/06. The next season they would again sign a central midfielder, bringing in Michael Ballack on a free transfer.

It is quite possible these players wouldn't have arrived at Stamford Bridge if Mourinho had signed his real target. Steven Gerrard.

José Mourinho has said he tried to sign Steven Gerrard three times. 'He is one of my favourite enemies,' he said, in typical Mourinho style. He tried to sign Gerrard for Chelsea, for Inter Milan and then for Real Madrid. Gerrard has admitted that when Chelsea tried to sign him in 2005 he went as far as handing in a transfer request before eventually signing a new contract.

The achievement and emotion of Liverpool's win in Istanbul threw a veil over the prospects of the club. Liverpool were well behind Manchester United, Arsenal and Chelsea in terms of both the quality of the playing staff and the resources. Abramovich arriving had ignited the transfer market in a way Liverpool could not contend with. In simple terms, the clear path to success lay at Stamford Bridge. Anfield offered hopes and dreams, but Stamford Bridge dripped silver and gold. The logical choice for any footballer would have been Chelsea, but Steven Gerrard chose with his heart, logic be damned.

If Gerrard signs for Chelsea they have to overcome one of English football's great mantras. Gerrard and Lampard can't play together. They are too similar. Sven-Göran Eriksson's inability to get the best out of them was why his England side were never successful.

Tactically Eriksson had a preference for a 4-4-2 system everywhere he went. He had great success with it, winning trophies and titles around Europe. The issue with the 4-4-2 is that it can easily be overrun in midfield, especially with two attack-minded players. While Gerrard had defensive capabilities his strongest assets were going forward, likewise with Lampard. To place the reins on either of them would mean not getting the maximum from either player. Add into the selection mix Beckham, Scholes and Joe Cole, and the 4-4-2 is a hindrance.

Putting aside the relative merits of the other players in the squad, a change of system would be required to get the best out of a Gerrard–Lampard axis. Their strengths require a player behind them to protect the space that they would invariably leave. Mourinho's Chelsea were perfectly designed to provide this. Claude Makélélé's ability to protect the space between midfield and the defence was so revered that the role was named after him. Makélélé played as the deepest player in a Galactico midfield at Real Madrid, a midfield that included Figo, Zidane and Beckham, with Raúl and Ronaldo up front. It is fair to say he had to do more than one man's defensive work in that structure.

Mourinho did not use a 4-4-2, he utilised a 4-3-3 structure which would support Steven Gerrard and Frank Lampard's attacking strengths, while Makélélé covered their forward runs, retaining defensive security.

Gerrard's presence on the right side of the central midfield would not only bring his drive and creative, goalscoring abilities in central areas. Robben was a wide player who drove infield from the left side. Gerrard was highly capable of positioning himself wide on the right when the situation demanded. With his quality of delivery Didier Drogba and Frank Lampard's opportunities to score would only increase.

A few years later José Mourinho had left the club. Carlo Ancelotti would eventually arrive and win the Premier League in 2010. Ancelotti's preference was for a diamond formation, which would further accentuate the axis of Lampard and Gerrard. Ashley Cole's overlaps plus the movement from in to out of Malouda provided the width on the left. Ivanovic provided width on the right with a static presence. Gerrard's dynamism might have improved the threat on Chelsea's right, even for a team that notched over 100 league goals.

At Euro 2004 England were supremely talented but struggled to get the best out of their midfield unit. Paul Scholes was often shunted to the wing, in a position from which he could not influence the game. Had Eriksson played to the strengths of his central players, dropping Beckham from the side and going to a diamond shape, he might have got the best out of Gerrard and Lampard, as well as Paul Scholes. It is arguable that England did not get the best out of these three players because of a focus on getting the best out of a single player, David Beckham.

There are other solutions to the problem that retains Beckham, such as moving to a 3-5-2 and playing Beckham as right-wing-back, but this involves leaving out Scholes, a player who is often described as superior to Gerrard and Lampard. The illustrations show that for both club and country the right manager would have no issues successfully playing Gerrard and Lampard together. Gerrard might not have scored quite as many goals, but the same could be said for Lampard, given that both took free kicks and penalties for their clubs, though both would still have scored with regularity.

What would this have meant for Gerrard? Of course his Liverpool legacy would be in tatters, but he would have at least two Premier League wins to his name and another Champions League. Whether Chelsea themselves would have been even more successful is debatable, as in 2008 Manchester City were taken over by Sheikh Mansour and their success was almost as inevitable as Chelsea's. Football at large would certainly have had the privilege of seeing one of the great midfield pairings on a weekly basis, one that would have become as renowned as Xavi and Iniesta.

WHAT IF BRIAN CLOUGH
HAD MANAGED ENGLAND?

On 17 October 1973 a goalkeeper called Jan Tomaszewski had the game of his life in a World Cup qualifier for Poland against England at Wembley. At half-time, in a TV studio, a famous football manager called him a 'clown' and urged the nation's fans not to worry. The Polish had taken the lead through Jan Domarski but Allan Clarke had equalised from the spot. For the next forty-five minutes Tomaszewski was inspired. The ball simply would not go in the Polish net. The game finished 1-1 and England had failed to qualify for the World Cup.

Soon after, Sir Alf Ramsey, the man who had guided England to victory in the 1966 tournament, was sacked. Many English football fans wanted the man in the studio to take over. His name was Brian Clough and he had already guided Derby County to the First Division title through his meteoric rise in football management. In their wisdom, the FA decided to give the job to Clough's arch-rival at the time, Don Revie. Revie had established Leeds United as the dominant team in English football, and on paper had all the credentials, but Clough had charisma, and would have been a popular choice with the fans.

Revie's first task was to qualify for the 1976 European Championships, but England were drawn in a tough group featuring both Czechoslovakia and Portugal. They started brightly with a 3-0 victory over the Czechs at Wembley, but when they lost the return fixture, qualification was no longer a formality. A 1-1 draw with Portugal in Lisbon saw Czechoslovakia come through and take the group. The fact that the Czechs were a fine side that actually went on to win the tournament cut no ice with the FA. It was seen as yet another failure.

Revie's England faced another tough qualification group as they sought to make the 1978 World Cup finals. They were unseeded and were placed in a group with the long-established proven winners, Italy. In the early games against Finland and Luxembourg, England laboured to victory. Revie's England failed to replicate the dominance that his Leeds team had enjoyed. England fans thought his sides too defensive, his team selections too inconsistent. A 2-0 defeat to Italy in Rome saw Revie come under pressure. In July 1977, with two games still left in the qualification group, Revie sensationally quit as England manager.

This time, the clamour for Brian Clough to take over, both in the press and among England fans, had reached fever pitch. Since the infamous night against Poland, Clough's career had been a switchback ride. When Revie left Leeds for England, Clough took over at Elland Road for an ill-fated 44 days, before being sacked. But now, Clough was back. He had guided Nottingham Forest from the depths of Division Two to the top of Division One. On 5 December, Clough was interviewed by the FA at Lancaster Gate. He was outspoken across a range of issues, not just those concerning football. He had outstanding, if at times unorthodox, man-management skills which brought the very best out of his players. He was outperforming his rivals at the 'big clubs' every week. And he was quite happy to let them know.

The polite parlance for what happened in the interview with the FA is that it was a 'frank exchange of views'. The FA didn't have the nerve to appoint Clough. They went for Ron Greenwood, a decent coach, and seen by many as a 'safe pair of hands'. As Clough said years later, 'I'm sure England's selection committee thought I'd want to run the whole damn show. They were shrewd then, because that's exactly what I would have done.' It was an opportunity missed. A chance to give arguably the finest English manager of all time the opportunity to mould the national team to greatness.

But what if the FA had been bold? What if they had appointed Brian Clough as the manager of the England football team?

Clough reaches an agreement with the FA that Peter Taylor stays at Nottingham Forest until the end of the season, but is allowed to join him for England games. He remains on the phone to his most trusted football friend and advisor throughout the rest of the season and Taylor guides Forest to the Division One title. Clough gathers the England squad together for his first game in charge, which is a friendly against West Germany at the Olympic Stadium in Munich. He tells them that with the talent they have in the squad they are a disgrace for not qualifying for the World Cup in Argentina. The squad reacts differently. Some respond. Some don't. England play with much more attacking intent, with wide players Coppell and Barnes always lively, and Keegan a waspish threat up front. The West Germans edge the game 2-1. There are many positive signs, but Clough makes some big early decisions. He is not convinced by the midfield duo of Wilkins and Brooking and he comes to a decision on the goalkeeping position. As he explained, 'Shilton was head and shoulders above Clemence. Alternating the two was a massive insult to Shilton.'

Clough's first big qualification campaign is for the European Championships of 1980. England are drawn in a group that features both Ireland teams, Bulgaria and Denmark. Many of the England squad are drawn from the Liverpool team that Clough had battled against in Division One. He looks to youth, players who show no fear, who are not weighed down by the three lions on their shirt. The young, dynamic West Brom midfielder Bryan Robson is drafted into the squad. Viv Anderson from Clough's old team Nottingham Forest becomes one of the first black players to play for England. He is joined by another black player from the exciting West Brom team, Laurie Cunningham. Kenny Sansom takes over from an ageing Mick Mills at left-back. Clough gives the captaincy to Kevin Keegan, who is happy with his manager's unequivocal approach. A number of attacking options are tried alongside Keegan, including Bob Latchford and Stuart Pearson, before Clough settles on Tony Woodcock, another of his old Forest team.

Clough tells Trevor Francis that if he wants to be part of the England set-up he has to stop playing in America. Francis ends his time on loan at Detroit Express. With a rest in the summer months and a good pre-season, Francis becomes less injury-prone. The England squad begins to take shape. It reflects the manager's character. Bold, incisive, yet also pragmatic and effective. England breeze through the qualification rounds with a 100 per cent record. Shilton keeps a clean sheet in every game at Wembley. Centre-halves Phil Thompson and Dave Watson take great pride in those clean sheets. The central midfield of Robson and Terry McDermott has energy, dynamism and an eye for goal.

Clough ruffles feathers when he ditches the Admiral football strip for the finals. 'A Rolls-Royce is always a Rolls-Royce and it's the same with the England strip. There's no need to mess about with it.' The plain white shirts are back.

England arrive in Italy in good spirits. Clough takes the team on a walkabout tour of Rome. Outside the

Vatican the FA tour managers get nervous when Clough talks about 'turning water into wine' at Forest.

It is a relaxed squad ahead of the opening game against Belgium in Turin. Clough chooses an attacking line-up with Coppell, Keegan, Woodcock and Cunningham up front. Trevor Francis has a slight knock and is ruled out. Belgium have come through a tough qualifying group that included Scotland, but they cannot live with England. Robson and McDermott dictate the tempo of the game and Coppell and Cunningham torment the Belgian full-backs Gerets and Renquin. After 20 minutes Robson plays a one-two with Keegan and bursts into the box. The Belgian keeper Pfaff blocks his shot but the ball breaks to the captain and Keegan gives England the lead. Belgium show just why they won their group as they try to assert themselves in the second half, but Thompson and Watson stand firm, and Shilton handles everything with great confidence. After 65 minutes Cunningham's pace is too much for Gerets and his cross finds the head of Woodcock, who puts England in command. They see out the game comfortably to make the perfect start.

England stay in Turin to take on hosts Italy three days later. After having some dubious decisions in this city against Juventus with Derby County seven years earlier, Clough says he is pleased to see that the referee is from Romania. The England manager shows his pragmatic side when he drafts in the experience of the Liverpool players to his squad. Phil Neal comes in at right-back for Anderson, and despite his glittering display against Belgium, Laurie Cunningham is replaced by Ray Kennedy.

The stadium in Turin is a cauldron as Italy kick off. Baresi and Collovati are making their presence felt with some typical Italian defending. Keegan and Woodcock are on the receiving end of some 'robust' tackling. The England defence retains its discipline at the other end and the teams go in all-square at the break. In the second half England begin to gain control as McDermott and Kennedy combine well in midfield. Bryan Robson stays more as a shield in front of the back four rather than marauding forward in his usual style. Dino Zoff in the Italian goal thwarts both Keegan and Woodcock with outstanding saves.

There are just eight minutes left when Keegan holds the ball up on the edge of the Italian area and lays it off to McDermott. With a neat dummy McDermott loses Gentile and then fires in an unstoppable drive from 20 yards that not even Zoff can keep out. It will later win goal of the tournament. It sparks pandemonium on the England bench as Clough and Taylor punch the air. Yet the drama is not over. There are less than two minutes left when Watson is adjudged to have pushed Benetti from a corner. It seems a harsh decision. Tardelli steps up and hits the penalty firmly and to the right. But Shilton pulls off a brilliant one-handed save. England hold out and are top of the group.

Trevor Francis is now fully fit and is the only change to the team that beat Italy as England face Spain in their last group fixture. They need only a draw to go straight through to their first major final since 1986. West Germany have topped Group One after wins against Czechoslovakia and the Netherlands and a draw with Greece. Clough says that it has been 'too long' and that he and his team are ready to give the nation what it has craved for 14 long years.

It takes only eight minutes for England's new-found confidence to be tested. Phil Neal trips Vicente del Bosque in the area and the referee points to the spot. Dani steps up and this time Shilton goes the wrong way. England are shaken and struggle to find their rhythm. At half-time Clough calls on his team to keep calm and keep playing. Within five minutes of the restart Kennedy clips in an inviting cross that looks to have eluded everyone until Francis's electric pace sees him arrive at the far post to drill in the equaliser. England know a draw will see them into the final, and now their confidence returns. Keegan sets up Woodcock to give his side the lead, and with seven minutes remaining the England captain bravely heads in a cross from Francis.

It is a proud moment for Brian Clough as he leads his team out for the 1980 European Championship Final against West Germany. On the morning of the game he has taken the team to the Colosseum. 'Now that was real pressure,' says the England manager. 'This is just another game of football.' Clough goes on to say he has the greatest respect for the West German team and is a big admirer of Karl-Heinz Rummenigge. Yet the confidence he has in his own team is absolute.

```
                Keegan        Woodcock


   R. Kennedy                              Francis
                McDermott     Robson

      Sansom       Watson     Thompson   Anderson
                        Shilton
```

Straight from the kick-off the tempo of the game is full throttle as both teams look to establish control. The West German wing-back has early success down their left-hand side and Shilton has to be at his best to keep out a header from Hrubesch. Bryan Robson has his hands full keeping tabs on Rummenigge but Schuster and Müller are not used to the intensity of McDermott and the physicality of Kennedy. The game is finely poised at half-time.

As the teams return for the second half the England fans see that Clough has taken off Trevor Francis and replaced him with Steve Coppell. England look to be more compact and have Woodcock and Keegan working tirelessly in the channels to exploit the spaces behind the West German wing-backs. Coppell and Kennedy give extra support to full-backs Anderson and Sansom, so that the supply to the West German forwards has been effectively reduced. The wing-backs are crossing from deep and Shilton is in full command of his area. Now it is England's turn to take control and they camp in the West German half after the hour mark. After 72 minutes, Steve Coppell forces a corner on the right and takes it himself. The ball is only half-cleared as the West German defence pushes out. Terry McDermott chips in a delightful ball towards the penalty spot. Schumacher rushes out but Keegan bravely just beats him to the ball and heads home. The England captain doesn't see the ball go in the net, but is mobbed on the floor by his team-mates.

With Keegan clearly still troubled by the clash with Schumacher, Clough replaces him with the young Nottingham Forest striker Garry Birtles. England now look to play on the counter. They retain their compact shape. Birtles and Woodcock work tirelessly up front, chasing lost causes and pressing the West German defence. There are just three minutes left when West Germany are awarded a free kick five yards outside the box. Bernd Schuster curves his shot over the England wall and it arrows towards the top corner until Shilton's fingertips take it over the bar. It is West Germany's last clear chance. Nicolae Rianea, the Romanian referee, blows his whistle and sparks scenes of joy on the England bench and behind their goal. Brian Clough is the calmest person in the stadium and playfully slaps Kevin Keegan on the cheek to see if he is fit enough to go up for the trophy.

England are European champions. Brian Clough has delivered exactly what the FA wanted.

The new Prime Minister, Margaret Thatcher, welcomes the team to a party at 10 Downing Street, after an open-top bus tour of the capital. Clough asks Mrs Thatcher to 'take a look at unemployment'. The FA blazers fix their smiles. 'We'll enjoy this moment,' says Clough, 'but now for the big one.'

England have a swagger about them that comes from being champions of Europe. There is an off night in Switzerland, but England top the group, beating Hungary, Romania and Norway. Clough stays loyal to the squad from Italy, but he has two main problems to solve in the spine of his team. His captain, Keegan, and centre-half, Watson, are now in their 30s. Clough adds Butcher from Ipswich and Withe from newly crowned European champions Aston Villa.

Bryan Robson scores the fastest ever goal at a World Cup Finals when he volleys in against France after just 13 seconds. England go on to win their opening game 3-1 and top their group, with further wins against Czechoslovakia and Kuwait. The brilliant but brittle Trevor Francis has picked up a knock against the Czechs and sits out the game against Kuwait. He is a major doubt for the next phase.

The second round of group games sees England paired with Spain and old adversaries West Germany, who are up first. With Francis still not fit, Clough brings in Peter

Withe to partner Tony Woodcock up front. Both sides are too wary of each other. There is little goalmouth action at either end and the game finishes in a 0-0 stalemate. West Germany then beat Spain 2-1 three days later. To progress to the semi-finals, England need to win by two clear goals.

Clough springs a surprise by drafting in the young Arsenal wide player Graham Rix to play on the left. Steve Coppell gives balance on the right and Francis is fit enough to partner Woodcock up front. Robson and McDermott patrol the central midfield. Spain know their chance of qualification has gone but prove obdurate opponents. There is no score at half-time. After an hour it looks like England have a lifeline when an inswinging corner from Rix is bundled in by Robson, but the referee disallows the goal for a push on the Spanish keeper Arconada. Clough takes off a tiring Francis and replaces him with Withe. There are just five minutes left when Spain force a rare corner. Butcher heads clear and Coppell starts a sweeping move upfield. Terry McDermott takes the Spanish centre-half out with a decoy run and Coppell finds Woodcock, who shoots. Agonisingly for England it hits the post. The 16-year wait for a second World Cup goes on. Clough is devastated. He vows to redouble his efforts.

In 1984 the country is in upheaval as the miners' strike begins. Clough is vocal in his support of the miners and donates personal cheques to the cause. The England team is in upheaval too, as Clough seeks to refresh his Euro 80-winning side. The FA may disapprove of his heart-onsleeve politics, but they know he is untouchable. Keegan and McDermott have served well and are thanked. Clough loses patience with the injury-prone Francis, especially as he now plays in Italy. Bryan Robson's body is showing signs of wear and tear.

England negotiate their group, after some anxious moments against Denmark, to give Clough a 100 per cent tournament qualifying record. They also travel over to France to get a taste of what is to come in the summer. Clough tries some different combinations. The Ipswich pair of Osman and Butcher are the centre-halves. Sammy Lee of Liverpool and Peter Reid of Everton offer options in midfield. The young Watford winger Barnes comes in with his striker team-mate Blissett. But Michel Platini is in irrepressible form for France and scores both goals in a 2-0 win.

England return to France four months later and meet the hosts in their first game. Clough knows he cannot afford to lose the opener and packs his midfield. Terry Fenwick sits in front of the back four and follows Platini everywhere. Lee, Robson and Reid play as a diamond with Robson ready to join the attack. Clough is still relying on his tried and trusted pair of Withe and Woodcock, who start up front. It is the French who play all the football, but with Butcher at the back in obdurate mood, and Shilton in prime form, England escape with a 0-0. In the second game against Yugoslavia, Clough loosens the reins and brings in Barnes on the left, with Sammy Lee moving out to the right. England win 1-0 with a goal from Woodcock, but it is a less than thrilling display. Clough bristles at the press conference and talks about 'getting the job done'.

A draw against Belgium in the final game will see England through to the semi-finals. Bryan Robson is missing with a knock, so the England midfield is even more pedestrian. Belgium can go through themselves if they win. Again it is the England back four that stands firm, with Anderson, Sansom, Butcher and Fenwick all producing outstanding displays. Blissett replaces a tiring Withe after an hour, and Barnes has some good moments, but it is the Belgians who collapse in disappointment at the 0-0 scoreline when the referee blows his whistle.

England's game management has been the feature of their performances so far, but in the semi-final against Spain they need something more. Bryan Robson is fit again and comes back into midfield with Lee and Reid. Withe is left out and Blissett starts alongside Woodcock and Barnes up front. The Spanish play with Maceda as sweeper in front of Señor, Salva and Camacho. In Arconada they have a keeper every bit as confident as Shilton. Again the defences of both teams dominate, but it is an intriguing match-up. At the end of 120 minutes nothing can separate the sides at 0-0. The match goes to penalties. Shilton can do nothing as Spain confidently score each of their five. Luther Blissett blazes England's third penalty over the bar and there is no repeat of the Euro 80 success.

By the time the 1986 World Cup arrives, Brian Clough has had eight years as England manager. The glory of the 1980 European Championships win has started to fade. Clough's reputation for attractive, attacking football is being questioned by the press. They clamour for the inclusion of flair players like Glenn Hoddle and Chris Waddle, but after trying them in low-profile friendly games, Clough continues to leave them out. The biggest surprises in his World Cup squad are two young Nottingham Forest players, Des Walker and his own son Nigel. 'These young men have had exceptional seasons and the experience will be good for them in the future. I would have no hesitation in calling on either in this World Cup,' said Clough when questioned. The mood in the England camp is more serious. There are no walkabouts in Mexico.

England begin their campaign in pedestrian fashion with yet another 0-0 draw against Portugal. 'We cannot win the World Cup in our first game, but we can certainly lose it,' says Clough as the press get even more restless. In the next game against Morocco, England take an early lead through Butcher, who heads home a corner. Then disaster strikes as Robson goes down with an injury to his shoulder. The England midfield is disrupted. A rare Moroccan shot deflects off Butcher and wrong-foots Shilton. England stutter. The game ends 1-1.

The pressure on Clough is mounting. He becomes even more prickly. 'I just happen to think I might know more about the game than you,' he replies to press questions. The final game against Poland is now a must-win. With Robson out injured, Clough brings in Steve Hodge of Aston Villa alongside Peter Reid. Trevor Steven of Everton and John Barnes start on the wings. Division One top scorer Gary Lineker is paired with Newcastle's Peter Beardsley up front. The side has a much more attacking look to it. England are on the front foot from the start and Lineker scores inside ten minutes. By half-time he has completed a hat-trick and England are coasting. The 3-0 win takes them through to the knockout stage. 'Sometimes you win football matches in unusual places,' says Clough, 'like before you even set foot on the field.'

Paraguay is a different challenge in the last-16 knockout stage. Clough brings in Gary Stevens of Tottenham to bolster the midfield, leaving John Barnes on the bench. But England carry their confidence from the Poland victory into the game. The understanding between Beardsley and Lineker seems telepathic, and they have Paraguay on the back foot from the start. Lineker scores before half-time, Beardsley just after and Lineker seals the win with 15 minutes to go. Clough is almost back to his old chipper self in the press conference. He is asked if his side can beat Argentina in the quarter-finals. 'We beat them a couple of years ago when it really mattered, so I don't see why not,' answers Clough as FA blazers watch on, anxiously hoping for no more mentions of the Falklands.

The quarter-final against Argentina is an epic struggle. Clough's team are focused and obdurate in the first half, and Lineker has a couple of half-chances. Reid and Hodge have shackled Maradona. All to play for in the second half. Five minutes in and Maradona attacks from deep with a mazy dribble. On the edge of the box he aims to play a one-two with Burruchaga, but Steve Hodge sticks out a boot. The ball loops up towards goal. Maradona beats Shilton to the ball. The Argentinians go wild. The England team protest that he has used his hand. Despite replays clearly showing that he did, Maradona's goal stands. Clough's usual poker face gives way to pent-up frustration. Four minutes later Maradona scores the goal of the tournament with a dribble of consummate brilliance. Clough brings on Barnes for a last throw. The winger begins to torment the Argentinian defence. There is less than ten minutes to go when he crosses for Lineker to head home. England throw everything at the Argentinians, but the equaliser will not come. England are out.

Clough doesn't hold back at the press conference. 'The goal was a cheat. Maradona isn't a great player anymore. He is a cheat.' Clough is asked to explain what he means. 'Which part of cheating Argentinian do you not understand?' It is a position Clough maintains in his usual forthright manner. References are made to the Falklands War. The Prime Minister, Margaret Thatcher, becomes involved. The British government try to prevent further tensions rising by wishing Argentina good luck in the next round. They go on to win the competition. In the ITV studios, as a panellist for the final, Clough insists: 'That should have been us in the final.' Days later the FA thank him for his services and he is replaced by Bobby Robson. Rumours are rife that the decision was taken on the plane home from Mexico.

So what if the FA had appointed Brian Clough as the manager of the England national team in December of 1977? They would have hired a manager at the height of his powers. A man that at times bordered on genius. A man that at times bordered on the absurd. He would have divided players, football writers and fans alike. He would have kept the FA in a state of constant anxiety. But that is what made Brian Clough, Brian Clough. And there has been no one like him, before or since.

WHAT IF AJAX NEVER SOLD?

De Toekomst is the envy of world football.

The Ajax Amsterdam academy has developed a stream of footballing talent. They have not just produced a single world-class talent, or a batch of talents, but decades'-worth of global stars.

Ajax Amsterdam's history stretches back to 1900. Though the club did not become professional until the 1960s, with the foundation of the Eredivisie in 1956 Ajax became semi-professional. Part-timers. Ajax had won several national championships prior to the foundation of the Eredivisie, many of them won by English manager Jack Reynolds. Reynolds managed Ajax from 1915–25 and then from 1928 until 1947, with two world wars interrupting his time at the club. Reynold spent much of World War Two as a prisoner of war. It was Reynolds who first introduced youth teams to Ajax, with the concept that they should be trained and coached in the same way as the first team.

In modern terms this would be considered ill-conceived as youth players are children, not mini adults, but by merely having youth teams in place Ajax were ahead of their rivals and the seeds planted for what was to come.

The journey towards total football continued with another Englishman arriving in Amsterdam to lay down a significant marker – Vic Buckingham. Buckingham had two spells as manager of Ajax, the first between 1959 and 1961, the second 1964–65. Buckingham instilled a 'push and run' style at Ajax. Most significantly, in his second spell Buckingham gave a debut to a 17-year-old Johan Cruyff.

Buckingham's replacement as Ajax manager was a man who had experienced the youth system introduced by Jack Reynolds and proceeded to score 122 goals for *de Godenzonen*, Rinus Michels.

Michels is viewed as the father of total football. Michels had a stroke of fortune that Ajax had a number of highly talented players waiting to emerge from the youth ranks and take the world by storm. In the second round of the 1966/67 European Cup, Michels and Ajax were drawn against Liverpool in the round of 16. In the thick Amsterdam fog the home side beat Liverpool 5-1. As well as Cruyff, Sjaak Swart and Wim Suurbier played in the game. They would have important roles in Ajax's rise. Significantly, Swart and Suurbier were also graduates of the Ajax youth system.

The training methods of Rinus Michels were also attracting the attention of outsiders. His approach was considered to be highly technical with the focus on ball control and players thinking for themselves on the pitch. The total football style required players who were versatile, comfortable in possession and who felt at ease in different areas of the pitch, free to move off the ball in the knowledge that team-mates would be intelligent enough to leave their position to cover them and also fit enough to apply extreme pressure to opponents in possession. The blueprint for the next half-century or more of football.

In 1968/69 Ajax would reach their first European Cup Final against AC Milan. Little did anyone know how intertwined Ajax, Milan and the European Cup would become. Milan easily beat Ajax 4-1 with Pierino Prato scoring a hat-trick, still the only one in a European Cup or Champions League Final.

Wim Suurbier, Barry Hulshoff, Anton Pronk, Sjaak Swart, Piet Keizer and Johan Cruyff all started in the 1969 European Cup Final. All came through the Ajax youth system.

Two years later many of the same players would face Panathinaikos in the 1971 European Cup Final. A young Arie Haan came off the bench in the second half to score the second goal and clinch the 2-0 victory. This was the dawn of an Ajax of global stars. Neeskens, Muhren, Haan and Cruyff would bewitch the global audience of the 1974 World Cup after sealing their European legacy with three consecutive European Cup wins. With each passing final another young Ajax player would emerge. In 1972 Ruud Krol moved into the starting line-up, having missed the previous final with a broken leg. Cruyff scored both goals for Ajax as they beat Inter Milan 2-0.

There was a change of manager following the first European Cup win. Rinus Michels departed for Barcelona (two years later Cruyff would join him). It is Michels' name that is most connected with Ajax but it was Ştefan Kovács who won two out of the Ajax triple European crowns. Kovács continued the total football style and promotion of youth.

In 1973 Ajax would defeat Juventus 1-0 in the final. The addition from the youth ranks, Johnny Rep, scored the only goal. After this third victory the Ajax generation began to break up. Piet Keizer retired in 1974. Cruyff joined Barcelona in 1973. Johan Neeskens joined Barcelona in 1974. Arie Haan went to Anderlecht in 1975. Johnny Rep also left in 1975, joining Valencia. Wim Suurbier signed for Schalke in 1977. Ajax were not a club capable of playing large wages and the Eredivisie was not a big league (this has not changed); the lure of Spain, Italy and Germany would be too much for this generation of stars.

By the 1980s Ajax were beginning a second surge of superstar talents which also yielded European trophy success, spilling into the early 90s.

Ajax reached back-to-back European Cup Winners' Cup Finals in 1987 and 1988.

In 1987 Ajax defeated Lokomotive Leipzig 1-0. The Ajax goalscorer was one Marco van Basten. A year later

Van Basten would be volleying a magnificent goal in a European Championship Final for the Netherlands having won the European Cup with AC Milan. Also in the Ajax team were youth graduates Frank Verlaat, John van 't Schip, Rob Witschge, Aron Winter and Frank Rijkaard. Sonny Silooy and Stanley Menzo were not youth graduates but Ajax signed them from their original clubs before they had made a first-team appearance.

As the transfer markets opened up Ajax used their scouting network to bring in young players early in their careers, adding to their already formidable youth set-up.

By the 1988 final loss to Mechelen, both Rijkaard and Van Basten were in Milan (with Ruud Gullit, signed from PSV and forming one of the most famed football trios of all time). The door was opened for John Bosman and another young forward, Dennis Bergkamp.

The 1992 UEFA Cup Final was the signal for the next mass exodus. Ajax beat Torino on away goals (UEFA Cup finals were played over two legs, with away goals counting double, another reason why the competition was considered one of the hardest to win). In the Ajax starting line-up were Frank de Boer (brother Ronald was not quite a first-team regular) and Bryan Roy in addition to Bergkamp and Winter. On the bench Edwin van der Sar served as back-up to Stanley Menzo. That summer the Italian teams raided Ajax. Aron Winter was signed by Lazio. John van 't Schip joined Genoa. The 1992 turnover continued as Foggia signed Bryan Roy. Gaping holes started to appear in the Ajax starting line-up, which were not helped in 1993 as Inter Milan swooped for Wim Jonk and at the same time took their big target, Dennis Bergkamp.

Ajax recruited smartly and promoted from within. By 1994/95 they were able to win the Champions League with a squad made up of youth products and clever recruits. Edwin van der Sar, Danny Blind, Winston Bogarde, Frank de Boer, Ronald de Boer, Michael Reiziger, Edgar Davids, Marc Overmars, Clarence Seedorf, Finidi George, Nwankwo Kanu, Patrick Kluivert, Jari Litmanen and the returning Frank Rijkaard. AC Milan were defeated 1-0 and these players would form the backbones of some of the biggest teams in Europe for the next decade. The greatest Ajax generation.

Ajax would not win another European trophy but they were not done with developing top-class international talent. Wesley Sneijder, Rafael van der Vaart, Nigel de Jong, Thomas Vermaelen, Jan Vertonghen, Toby Alderweireld, Donny van der Beek, Christian Eriksen and Mathijs de Ligt all came through. In addition Zlatan Ibrahimovic, Luis Suárez and Frenkie de Jong were signed early in their careers, benefitting hugely from the Ajax finishing school.

Ajax have provided European football with their key stars, but what if Ajax were able to keep their stars?

In the 1970s little could have been done to retain the talent. Ajax could not compete financially. The same could be true of the 1980s and early 1990s exodus.

However, the talent drain did not go to the huge clubs. Rijkaard and Van Basten moved to Milan and Bergkamp and Jonk moved to Inter, otherwise the players were not lured by European giants, unlike the post-Champions League sales. Had Ajax found a way to hold off Milan and Inter until the Champions League era and the huge financial opportunities that came with it, just how strong could they have been?

As Marco van Basten left Ajax Dennis Bergkamp was starting to play in the first team. They played a few games together for Ajax but played numerous times for the Dutch national team. A Bergkamp and Van Basten strike partnership would have been a handful for any team in European football. The steel of Rijkaard would have been complemented by the silk of Aron Winter. Wouters and Blind were a very tough pair of defenders. Muhren, Witschge, van 't Schip and Bosman added sufficient quality that Ajax would certainly be challenging for European Cups.

At the same time Ajax's great rivals PSV were winning the European Cup. After a 0-0 draw with Benfica went to penalties PSV were the 1988 European champions. They capitalised on this success with the backing of their owners (Philips) and the 1987 sale of Ruud Gullit to AC Milan providing funds. They spent out on Romario. While not as rich as Serie A or La Liga or Ligue 1 (Marseille were embarking on a spending spree) there was money in the Eredivisie. Ajax would not have needed to find funds for transfers, but the wages to retain first Rijkaard and Van Basten, then Bergkamp and Jonk.

Not selling Rijkaard and Van Basten has a huge impact on AC Milan. Without this pair they probably don't win the 1989 and 1990 European Cups. With Rijkaard and Van Basten, plus Bergkamp and the others, Ajax likely win at least one of these tournaments. Milan's 1989 title is handed to Ajax. Milan's biggest result was beating a very good Real Madrid side in the semi-final, crushing them 5-0 in Madrid. Both Rijkaard and Van Basten scored in that game. Ajax could have beaten them and also seen off Steaua Bucharest, who Milan beat 4-0 in the final. Ajax add the 1989 European Cup to their three triumphs of the 1970s.

As time passes the Ajax squad grows stronger. By the start of the first Champions League season the squad consists of:

Stanley Menzo	Edwin van der Sar	Danny Blind
Jan Wouters	Sonny Silooy	Frank Rijkaard
Michael Reiziger	Frank de Boer	Aron Winter
Wim Jonk	Edgar Davids	Ronald de Boer
Clarence Seedorf	Bryan Roy	Rob Witschge
Marco van Basten	Dennis Bergkamp	Jari Litmanen
John van 't Schip	John Bosman	Marc Overmars

Some of the big names (Van der Sar, Reiziger, Davids, Seedorf) would not yet be ready to be first-team regulars. With players ready to come in and take places this now means that Ajax can sell at the time of their choosing.

Louis van Gaal could use his favoured 3-4-3 diamond formation:

Van Basten   Bergkamp   Overmars

Litmanen   Winter
      Jonk   Witschge

Rijkaard   Wouters   Blind

Menzo

The line-up is extremely strong, though it possibly lacks the balance and fluidity of the 1994/95 Champions League winners, particularly with wide central defenders also able to play as full-backs. Ajax would be able to go deep into the competition and the firepower of Van Basten, Bergkamp and Litmanen would overwhelm many teams around Europe, making Ajax five-time European champions and holders of the very first Champions League trophy.

Two seasons later Ajax win again. The 1994/95 squad has immense depth but now we add more striking power.

Ajax can choose to sell on the older players to create pathways for the younger players. Van 't Schip, Bosman, Wouters, Witschge, Silooy and Menzo are all over or around 30. Ajax likely could have sold them on in the knowledge that what was emerging was more than good enough. At Milan Marco van Basten spent much of the 1992/93 season injured; it was the injury that cut his career short.

We are going to imagine that Van Basten is fit and at the apex of his powers in 92/93 and he would only be 31 years old in 1994/95. The Ajax squad, already strong enough to win the Champions League, now looks like this:

Van der Sar F	de Boer	Blind	Rijkaard
Bogarde	R de Boer	Winter	Jonk
Davids	Seedorf	Roy	Musampa
Finidi George	Van Basten	Bergkamp	Litmanen
Overmars	Kanu	Kluivert	Reiziger

If Ajax no longer sell their players on, this squad of players is strong enough to win the Champions League again in 1996 (as it was they lost the final on penalties to Juventus after a 1-1 draw. Juventus then lost the next year's final to Dortmund.) By 1998 a number of the players would have retired, but within a couple of seasons their replacements will have emerged. Rafael van der Vaart debuts in 2000. Zlatan debuts in 2001. Wesley Sneijder debuts for Ajax in 2002. Zlatan remained playing at the top level of European football until after the age of 40. In theory he could have led the line for Ajax for 20 years. All 500-plus club goals scored in his career would have been scored in an Ajax shirt.

It was not until the mid to late 2000s that a group of quality defenders emerged from the Ajax youth ranks, but given their Champions League hat-trick in the mid-90s now comes at the height of the impact of Champions League money (before huge TV deals sweep Europe's domestic leagues) they would be operating as a superclub within a small league. They could easily use the riches to invest in defenders until the wave of Alderweireld, Vertonghen and Vermaelen come through.

As Litmanen, Bergkamp and Overmars drift out of the team Ajax suddenly find themselves with a forward line of Sneijder, Van der Vaart, Zlatan and, signed in 2007, Luis Suárez. The strength of those four attacking players in combination plus the depth of squad Ajax have by the early 2010s gives them a platform to compete against even the richest of European clubs.

If Ajax never have to sell their players it is quite likely that they have seven or eight European Cups/Champions Leagues to their name and some of the biggest teams in Europe find their tally diminished. Not only would the Ajax academy be the envy of Europe, but so would their trophy cabinet.

What might seem like the brightest timeline for Ajax could also develop into a dark mirror. Ajax's faith in youth development is a part of the club's deeper-rooted values. They may be the biggest and most commercially successful club in the Netherlands but their consumerism pales in comparison to the giants of European football.

If Ajax have eight European Cups they are undoubtedly one of those giants. With their domestic and Champions

League dominance Ajax would need a bigger challenge to satisfy themselves. A competition to truly test themselves and have the fans clamouring to watch every week.

Ajax push for the European Super League.

They push for it year after year.

Whether they succeed in getting the league isn't important. Their push is a symbolic shift away from the club's values and principles. The Dutch can go to war with each other over far less.

During the 2010s Ajax was a club feuding with itself. Legends Cruyff and Van Gaal went to battle over the direction the club should head in. It began over who the club should sign. Then spread to how to judge young players and the battle of data-led recruitment versus using experience and judgement. Tactically Cruyff described van Gaal as 'militaristic' while he wanted players to 'think for themselves'. The war split the club asunder for half a decade. During this period other clubs took Ajax's share of domestic honours.

The splits and damage caused by chasing the European Super League would be even more devastating. Key figures behind the scenes would leave. First-team stars slowly drift away from the behind-the-scenes chaos, slowly the club would be stripped of its on- and off-field talent, defeated by its new-found desire for excess.

The giant that grew too tall.

WHAT IF FOOTBALL HAD
A LINEAR CHAMPION
LIKE BOXING?

Everyone knows that Uruguay were the first football world champions.

Right?

Except …

Except that at the 1908 London Olympic Games the football associations organised a football tournament. Great Britain were the winners and arguably the first world champions at an event that featured Denmark, France, the Netherlands, Sweden and Great Britain. Hungary withdrew and France took their B team, who Denmark destroyed 17-1. At the second tournament, also won by Great Britain, there were 11 teams, all from Europe. After a war-related interlude the Olympics returned in 1920, with Belgium triumphant at another tournament with a distinctly European flavour.

So far, so Euros.

In 1924 this changed with Egypt, Uruguay and USA entering the mix. Uruguay would emerge victorious. In 1928 Mexico, Chile and Argentina were added, and

Uruguay would triumph again, beating Argentina 2-1 in a replayed final. Two years later at the first FIFA-organised World Cup the same two teams would face each other, Uruguay winning 4-2. In 1928 the Olympic tournament had 17 participants. The World Cup in 1930 had only 13 teams.

The Olympic football tournaments ran alongside the World Cup for almost a decade before another war interlude. In 1950 the true separation between Olympic champions and world champions occurred, with the world title elevated beyond the Olympic, a status that has been unchanged ever since.

Some teams still took each tournament equally seriously, especially the Eastern bloc nations that prevented their players from playing as professionals. Their amateur status meant that the Hungarian team that won the 1952 Olympics was the same line-up that crushed England twice in 1953 and then lost in the 1954 World Cup Final. The USSR side that won in 1956 had a certain Lev Yashin in goal.

Yet it remained clear who the champions of the world were. The winners of the World Cup. In 1966 Geoff Hurst had a goal awarded by a linesman and then 'some people were on the pitch' and it was all over. A year later Denis Law, Bobby Lennox and Jim McCalliog struck at Wembley to beat England 3-2. Two late Jack Charlton and Geoff Hurst goals could not save the game for England. The 'Wembley Wizards' claimed their place in football folklore. One month later Celtic would become the first British team to win the European Cup. Scottish fans and media could not help but declare themselves world champions, at the peak of the global game. The concept of a linear world champion has been a major discussion point in boxing for quite some time. As the number of belts grew and the championships waxed and waned in value, boxing historians followed the lineage. Who is the true champion? Who is the man who actually beat the man?

For football world champions the title is not on the line. Scotland were not world champions and the Jules Rimet trophy remained tucked away safely at the Football Association, until the next tournament, despite Scotland having beaten 'the man'. At one time world champions automatically qualified for the next tournament, but having to qualify along with the rest of the world meant they could lose their title without even being at the tournament. Only in 1990 (Argentina) and 1998 (Brazil) have the world champions lost their crown on the pitch, in the actual final. In 1970 England were beaten by the eventual winners Brazil during the group stage and in 1982 Italy beat the 1978 winners Argentina in the complex and never repeated double group stage tournament.

Efforts have been made to track who the linear world football champions are. In April 2022 the linear and actual champions were the same team, France, who took the linear championship from Spain in 2021's UEFA

Nations League following their 2018 World Cup success. According to the rankings Scotland are winners of 86 linear championship matches, England 73 linear wins and Argentina have 62 linear wins. Australia, Israel, South Korea, Turkey and Venezuela hold one linear championship each. As do the mighty Curacao.

This, of course, is not how football world championships work. The Olympics is not the World Cup. The world crown is not a belt to be defended in a ring. Or arena. Or stadium.

What if it was?

As the two championships were aligned before the 2022 World Cup this would have been an ideal time to start defending the championship. According to the lineage France have had four successful title defences, seeing off the threat of Kazakhstan, Finland, Ivory Coast and South Africa. Of course, their 'real' crown was not at stake. Had it been, these insignificant international fixtures would have been elevated to grand levels of importance. Viewers from around the world would tune in to see the world champions defend their title. The World Cup finals of 2010, 2014 and 2018 all topped 500 million television viewers. Whether 500 million people would tune in to watch Kazakhstan is another question.

These four games were in fact two World Cup qualifiers and two international friendlies. These fixtures might have looked somewhat more glamorous under a different system. Defending the title within a 'normal' schedule would hand shots at the world championship on an almost arbitrary basis, great for opportunity but terrible for concepts of fairness and merit. If the World Cup winners did not have to qualify for the next tournament the scheduling could be set aside for more significant events. FIFA has world rankings that are not considered to be of any great significance. However, if these were used to decide the next number one contender for a world title match-up, their importance would immediately be elevated. At the time of writing France's next fixture and next title defence is against Denmark. The highest-ranked team on the FIFA list is Brazil. If football was more like boxing the next world title clash would be a rerun of the infamous 1998 World Cup Final, a game in which the new champions dethroned the old. Zidane headed in two corners in front of a packed Stade de France and Paris turned blue.

When two heavyweight boxers clash the hype machine enters overdrive. For months there are interviews, predictions and theorising over the potential events ahead. Press conferences. Television specials. Documentaries. The stuff of legend. The public whipped into a frenzy over the 'hottest tickets in town'. One match-up at the centre of the universe.

These defences could not happen constantly, otherwise they would lose their magic. Four times a year would seem like a reasonable frequency, particularly outside of years with major tournaments. The current champions would need to come through 12 title defences plus a European Championship unscathed to retain their title.

What of the continental championships?

Should the world champions be from that championship they would have to defend it within the tournament. Should Brazil defeat France in the run-up to a Copa America their status would be under threat every time they played in the Copa. If they lost, the world championship could change hands multiple times on the way to the final until the winners of the Copa America would also be crowned as champions of the world.

To add further spice to the continental championships, the winners might automatically earn a world title match. If the world champions were from South America, the winners of the African Nations Cup would earn a match-up between their next continental tournament and the World Cup. The current CONCACAF Gold Cup winners are the USA, who would be in line for a world championship opportunity.

There have only been eight nations who have won the World Cup. Only eight world champions under the present system. Thirteen teams have reached the final. All eight have been from either Europe or South America, as have all 13 finalists. There have been 44 different teams who have been linear world champions, from South America, Europe, Asia, Africa, North America, Central America and Oceania. A system in which world champions had to defend their title on a regular basis would be a much more open shop. The negative would be that there would be far more world champions, but there would still be World Cup winners, and everyone would feel like they had more of a chance at being world champions. Pelé predicted an African winner of the World Cup by 2000, yet we still await the first. Meanwhile, Nigeria have won four linear world championship matches. As three-time African Nations Cup winners they would have had three title shots outside of World Cups. Egypt are seven-time Nations Cup winners, which would have earned them seven World Cup finals.

Imagine the spectacle of 75,000 people in the Cairo International Stadium to welcome France for a world championship match. The video packages have been rolled out for weeks. The imagery of Pharaohs versus Napoleon. The Pyramids and the Eiffel Tower. Mbappé versus Salah. A pre-game ceremony attended by the great and the good. Some not so great and not so good, such is the nature of these things. A dramatic fireworks display before the game. The pageantry of the national anthems, and finally the game is under way, with 500 million people tuned in. At half-time a global megastar performs. There will be people who only watch the game for the half-time show, just as they do with the Super Bowl. The second half is under way. Crucially the game is 90 minutes plus extra time, but there will be no penalties. Championship advantage comes into play. To paraphrase, to be the team, you have to beat the team.

At the final whistle another huge fireworks display, a trophy presentation, various interviews and speeches. The game event finally, slowly shuts down and the 75,000 drift off into the Cairo night, celebrating either as the newly crowned champions of the world or the still reigning, defending world champions.

Such a huge match in Cairo would be taking football out of its traditional strongholds and opening up the game, an excuse FIFA have used for holding tournaments in strange, unusual and ultimately dubious locations. The games could be held in neutral locations, especially if the match-ups are blockbusters. Club friendlies have shown that huge stadiums can be filled very easily with the right teams. Liverpool have played friendlies at the MCG in Australia, drawing crowds of 95,000 each time. How many fans could they attract for Brazil versus Argentina to decide the world championship?

The Egypt–France contest presented two global superstars. Brazil versus Argentina presents Neymar versus Messi plus a rich supporting cast. Never underestimate the importance of iconography when generating interest and those yellow Brazilian shirts vs the white and blue stripes of Argentina are a poster designer's dream. The sales pitch of the Brazilian carnival and the mythos of their *joga bonito* past far outweigh any reality of their actual quality. The queues for the box office would be round the block, Ticketmaster in meltdown. Never mind what could happen if the game was a PPV event. The potential revenue, if revenue is the most important thing, could be extraordinary. Factor in rematches, as there are in boxing, then you have the potential for a double blockbuster.

There is an argument that club football is bigger than international football. That Manchester United against Real Madrid to decide a world title would attract a larger audience than Brazil versus Argentina. The global television figures disagree. However, international football has certainly been diluted by the extraordinary quality of club football teams. If there is a best team in the world it is most likely to be a club team, not an international side with a seemingly endless stream of international mismatches. The concept of title matches would add meaning to international football, to the rankings and be something for all teams to play for, not just the select few.

WHAT IF THE MUNICH AIR CRASH NEVER HAPPENED?

On 1 February 1958 Arsenal took on Manchester United in front of 63,000 spectators at Highbury. United played scintillating football to lead at the break 3-0 through Edwards, Charlton and Taylor. In the second half Arsenal hit back, and in a frenetic few minutes were level with a goal from Herd and two from Bloomfield. Stung into a response, United regained the lead as Viollet and Taylor struck, before Tapscott pulled one back again for Arsenal. There were chances at both ends after this, but the current champions ran out 5-4 winners at the final whistle. Many who were there thought it the greatest First Division game of all. For the team nicknamed the 'Busby Babes' it was to be their last on English soil.

United's next match was in the European Cup, a quarter-final second leg against Red Star Belgrade. The 'Babes' were leading after a 2-1 win at Old Trafford. It was another thrilling game, ending in a 3-3 draw. United were now into the European Cup semi-finals for the second season in succession. After a difficult return journey from Prague in the previous round, the club chartered a

British European Airways flight from Belgrade. On the afternoon of 6 February the plane landed in Munich for refuelling. The pilot, Captain James Thain and co-pilot Captain Kenneth Rayment, made two abortive take-off attempts for England. With snow falling, the passengers disembarked from the plane and returned to the control tower. Thain was anxious to stay on schedule and decided to make a third attempt. The passengers took their seats once more. The plane set off and gathered speed but never achieved enough velocity for take-off. It skidded down the runway, crashed through a fence and hit the side of a house.

Twenty passengers died at the scene of the crash, including seven of the United team, Byrne, Taylor, Jones, Pegg, Whelan, Colman and Bent. Journalist, and former Manchester City and England goalkeeper, Frank Swift died on his way to hospital. Captain Kenneth Rayment died in hospital later that month. Duncan Edwards, thought by many to be the greatest English footballer of all time, died from his injuries in hospital on 21 February. The news of the crash was met with disbelief in Manchester and the whole city went into mourning. It was a disaster that would have a profound effect, not just on Manchester United, but on English football. So what if the ill-fated third attempt to take off had not happened and the 'Busby Babes' had flown home safely the next day?

There is no doubt that the United side that Busby had built had enraptured football fans not only in Manchester, but up and down the country. The youth of many of the side, the attacking verve, their fearless commitment against any opposition, had captured the imagination of all those whose ideal was the 'beautiful game'. Fans flocked to watch them wherever they played.

In 1958 the top tier of English football did not have the financial imbalance so prevalent today. There were still 'big clubs' and those clubs still had an advantage, but it was a more level playing field. Players were still on the 'maximum wage' and often stayed for long periods at one club. The format had remained unchanged since the first Football League in 1888, two points for a win and one point for a draw.

In the previous two seasons, United had won the First Division title and done so by 11 and 8 points, which in those days was a considerable margin. By the time they played Arsenal they were trailing Wolves by four points. United had made a slow start and had already lost seven games. In 1956/57 they lost only six games in their entire league campaign. Wolves went on to drop just another six points, with two defeats and two draws, from 1 February to the end of the season. United were clearly hitting their stride. Busby had introduced two exciting young wingers in Kenny Morgans and Albert Scanlon, who both survived the air crash. However, it is difficult to think they would have overhauled Wolves and won the title for a third year on the trot.

The 1958 FA Cup saw United ride to Wembley on a wave of emotion. With Matt Busby recovering from the air crash, Jimmy Murphy was interim manager. He made some astute short-term signings in Ernie Taylor and Stan Crowther. There is often talk of the 'romance' of the FA Cup, but fate was not to smile on United that year and they lost 2-0 in the final to Bolton Wanderers. With the side starting to hit top form in the league, and with Duncan Edwards and the rest of the 'Busby Babes' in full flow, United would surely have won the FA Cup that year.

United had been pathfinders in the European Cup. Matt Busby had the vision to see the value of the competition from its inauguration, and United entered despite stiff opposition from the FA. The previous year they had reached the semi-final at the first attempt, but lost 5-3 to eventual winners Real Madrid. They drew AC Milan in the semi-final in 1958 but although the revamped side won the home leg 2-1 they were soundly beaten in the return 4-0. The feeling was that the 'Busby Babes' were growing into the competition. They might well have beaten Milan. But it is a really tall order to suggest they would have beaten Real Madrid if they had met in the final. Madrid went on to win the competition in its first five years. United, with the young players gaining experience, could well have broken that run at some point. It is a really big 'if' because they would not have qualified for the European Cup in 1958/59. But given Matt Busby's quest, there is every chance United could have won the competition before they finally did in 1968.

The rivalry between United and Wolves had already been firmly established in the 1950s with the clubs taking six titles between them. Incredibly, United pushed Wolves to the title the season following the Munich air crash. It would be eight years before United would win the title again in 1965. So how many titles were the 'Busby Babes' denied? They would have run into the Spurs double-winning team, but it is more than likely they would have won a double themselves before Bill Nicholson's great team. Given any natural progression by the young United side, they would surely have proved too strong for Burnley in 1960 and Ipswich in 1962, despite Alf Ramsey's best efforts. The 'Busby Babes' were denied at least three additional First Division championships.

The cost of the Munich air crash to Manchester United is almost incalculable. The club lost its heart and soul, not just the eight players and the three backroom staff who died. But the tragedy also had a profound effect on the England national team. In the run-up to the 1958 World Cup, the United captain Roger Byrne had firmly established himself as the England left-back. Duncan Edwards had made his debut three years earlier at just 18 years and 183 days old, the youngest post-war England player until Michael Owen made his debut 43 years later. His reputation as a footballing colossus was already confirmed. The World Cup would be the perfect showcase for his talents. Tommy Taylor had secured his place as the England centre-forward and had already scored two hat-tricks for the national side.

What has to be remembered is that the England team at the time was chosen by the FA's 'selection committee'. The squad was then handed over to the manager, who at the time was Walter Winterbottom. The England under-23 squad was also a relatively new concept, having only been introduced in 1954. Edwards played in the first ever under-23 international against Italy aged just 17. But he was the exception. A 'young' England player was usually 21 or 22. With the age lowered to under-21s, nowadays players are much younger when they arrive in the full England side.

The England squad for the 1958 World Cup had been shaping up in the run-up to the tournament. Surprisingly, Edwards' partner at half-back for United, Eddie Colman, had not yet played for the under-23s, but he could very well have been called up for a 22-man squad. He was only 21 when he died yet he already had two Division One winners' medals. It was a similar story with centre-half Mark Jones. Many thought he could have played for England, but Billy Wright, the England captain at the time, blocked his path. David Pegg was very likely to have been chosen too, having already made his full England debut. It's quite possible United could have supplied six or seven players to the England squad in 1958, with three certain starters in Byrne, Edwards and Taylor.

So England travelled to Sweden for the World Cup, and despite the depleted squad the usual expectation accompanied them. On the surface, the fact is that England failed to get out of their group that contained eventual winners Brazil, Austria and the USSR. They started the tournament slowly, and were two down to the Soviet Union, before coming back strongly to equalise with goals from Taylor's replacement Derek Kevan and Tom Finney. In the next game they gained a fully deserved draw against Brazil, the only surprise being the 0-0 scoreline as both sides attacked throughout. England were rocked by an injury to Tom Finney, who despite being 36 was still one of the stars of world football. England knew that a win in the final group game against Austria would take them through to the quarter-finals, but with Finney again missing, they struggled to gain the initiative. They were twice behind and only by digging in, rather than playing well, did they come away with a 2-2 draw.

The result was that remarkably, both England and Russia had three points from three games, with an identical four goals for and four goals against. The only option was a play-off. England played much better than they had against Austria but this time luck eluded them as they went close to scoring on a number of occasions. The only goal of the game came from a poor goal kick from the England keeper McDonald which was intercepted by Ilyin. He traded passes with Voinov and Simonyan and slotted home off the post. England went close again but Russian keeper Yashin was imperious. England were out.

But what if Byrne, Edwards and Taylor had all played? How different would it have been?

There would have been no slow start against Russia. With Edwards driving the midfield England win the opening game. Taylor leading the line against Brazil may well have swung the outcome, but a draw still seems the most likely result. Knowing that a win against Austria would be enough to progress, England go through confidently with Edwards and Taylor both on the scoresheet.

In the quarter-finals England line up against Sweden. They had met in the Rasunda stadium in May 1956 and played out a 0-0 draw. Tom Finney was absent. Add the Preston maestro to the team, take Edwards at his barnstorming best, and know Taylor would put away any chances, and England edge the tie 2-1 and now play West Germany in the semi-finals. On the same European tour in 1956, England had played in Berlin and come away with a 3-1 win. It was one of Edwards' finest performances. England completely dominated the match, with the Germans scoring only a late consolation. England would have won again comfortably, 3-0, with two goals from Taylor and another from Finney.

The 1958 World Cup Final is now Brazil v England, the game the football world wants to see. Brazil have progressed to a 4-2-4 formation. Their forward line of

Garrincha, Vava, a 17-year-old Pelé and Zagallo is one of the finest in football history. Many in Brazil choose this team over the mesmeric team from 1970. England were still sticking to the WM formation, but the game in the group qualifiers had been close with both sides on the attack. The Munich air crash denied football one of its great games.

Vava opens the scoring for Brazil but Taylor equalises soon after and the teams go in at half-time 1-1. Brazil take command early in the second half with goals from Zagallo and Pelé. It looks like the Samba football will lead England a merry dance. Edwards rallies his team and after a slalom run strikes with an unstoppable left-footed shot to put the game in the balance again. Both sides give their all, but as the final whistle blows, Brazil edge another feast of attacking football 3-2.

The England squad for the 1962 World Cup contained many of the players who were to win the trophy four years later. Wilson, Moore and Charlton played; so did Jimmy Greaves. Roger Hunt was one of the 22 who travelled. Roger Byrne, by now 33, would have lost his place to Wilson. Tommy Taylor would have been 30, so might have still been in the squad, but likely as backup to Greaves. Eddie Colman would have been 25, arguably at his peak, and very likely to have been partnering Edwards in the England midfield instead of Ron Flowers or Bobby Robson. Big Duncan would surely have grown into one of the world's best footballers and have picked up at least one Ballon d'Or, given that Johnny Haynes, a fine player but no Edwards, finished third in 1961. Given that the England squad was clearly in transition, it is difficult to see them getting past the all-conquering Brazil side in the quarter-finals.

So on to the World Cup in England. Generation after generation of England fans have seen the iconic images of the 'Boys of 66' immortalised in their red shirts and forever the benchmark of the national team. In 1966 Duncan Edwards would have been 29, arguably at the peak of his powers. The way the game developed, the way he played, it is more than likely he would have dropped back to become a centre-half by this point. Ramsey's team had four world-class players in it – Charlton, Moore, Greaves and Banks. Add Edwards to that as a fifth. With Cohen and Wilson as full-backs, Edwards alongside Moore and Banks behind in goal, it is one of *the* great defensive units.

England swagger through the group without conceding a goal. Argentina are swept aside. A Eusébio

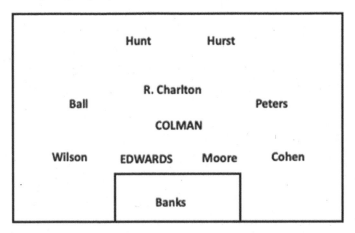

thunderbolt in the semi-final is the first goal England concede, but they win through. In the final, there is no drama, there is no extra time, there are no people on the pitch. England, led by their colossus of a captain, despatch West Germany 3-0.

If the aircraft does not make its ill-fated third attempt to take off along the runway in Munich on 6 February 1958, it is not Bobby Moore who takes the Jules Rimet trophy off the Queen on 30 July 1966. It is Duncan Edwards.

WHAT IF AN AFRICAN TEAM
WIN THE WORLD CUP?

François Omam-Biyik. 8 June 1990. Argentina 0
Cameroon 1.

The ball loops high into the Italian sky. It drops and
François Omam-Biyik leaps into the air, climbing over
the top of his Argentine marker. His downward header is
fumbled, slipping through the grasp of goalkeeper Nery
Pumpido and across the line. Cameroon take the lead
against the defending world champions, a lead they hold
until the final whistle. Cameroon shock the globe in the
opening game of the 1990 World Cup.

African nations competed in the football World Cup
from very early on. They debuted at the tournament
decades before England, as Egypt entered in 1934, the
second edition. At the time the competition was a straight
knockout. Unfortunately for Egypt they were drawn
against a strong Hungarian team. Their 4-2 defeat would
be the last African appearance at the World Cup until 1970.

Morocco drew their first game of the 1970 tournament
0-0 with Bulgaria but would lose their next two games.
African football had made very little impact on the

international stage. This would change in Germany in 1974, but for less positive reasons.

Zaire (DR Congo) would suffer defeats in all three games, losing 2-0 against Scotland, 9-0 against Yugoslavia and 3-0 against Brazil. The heavy losses were not what would live the longest in the memory, but a bizarre dead ball incident. Zaire conceded a free kick in their match against Brazil. Rivellino sets himself to strike the dead ball. The referee blows his whistle and Zaire's Mwepu Ilunga sprints from the defensive wall and smashes the ball as far away as he possibly can. It is indicative of attitudes towards Africa and African football that this was presented as 'African innocence' and 'naivety'. The truth is that Ilunga was unsurprisingly fully aware of the rules and merely frustrated to the point where he wanted to be sent off. The incident undoubtedly impacted the way a generation viewed African football.

At the next two tournaments African teams performed far more competitively. In 1978 Tunisia beat Mexico 3-1, lost 1-0 to Poland and drew 0-0 with West Germany. Algeria were victims of the complex tournament format in 1984. Algeria beat West Germany 2-1 in a major shock. They then lost 2-0 to Austria. After winning their final game 3-2 against Chile they had to watch on as Germany and Austria infamously played out a 1-0 West German win as both teams knew that this result would send them through. Cameroon also appeared at the tournament and drew all three group games, including a 1-1 with eventual champions Italy. Views of African football began to change.

In 1986 an African team progressed beyond the group stage for the first time. Morocco drew 0-0 with England and Poland in their group, then beat Portugal 3-1. They were then beaten 1-0 by West Germany.

Pelé's bold prediction that an African nation would win the World Cup in the 20th century seemed like it has some chance of coming true.

In 1990 Cameroon made their mark. The Italy tournament has a hallowed place in the memories of many but it was a dark, cynical tournament, filled with hard fouls, diving and time-wasting. Many of the innovations that have made football more entertaining were introduced due to the 1990 World Cup. The back pass laws were changed. The laws on tackling from behind changed. The professional foul and clear goalscoring opportunities entered the football lexicon due to on field actions in Italy.

Cameroon provided a technicolour high for the world. They were not above cynical fouls of their own, but they brought a joyous surprise element to the competition. Their victory against Argentina was followed by beating Romania 2-1. Cameroon were through after two games, meaning that the 4-0 thumping they received from the USSR had little meaning (interestingly four years later Russia would smash Cameroon 6-1, Oleg Salenko setting a World Cup record by scoring five times).

In the knockout round Cameroon faced Colombia. The game went to extra time and Cameroon goalkeeper René Higuita helped the Cameroonians into the next round. Roger Milla's first goal was a high-quality dribble and left-foot strike into the near top corner. His second goal was a gift, Higuita advancing from his penalty area to sweep up a long ball forward. There seemed to be no threat until Higuita began to dribble and exchange passes with a team-mate. The return pass produced a weak touch from Higuita. Cameroon pounced, allowing Milla to finish into an empty net. Cameroon progressed to face England in the quarter-finals.

England were heavily favoured and indeed came through the game, but in defeat Cameroon only served to cement their reputation. England had to fight to win through, requiring two hotly disputed penalties in order to edge the game 3-2. Cameroon led 2-1 with chances to extend their advantage until Lineker netted twin spot kicks.

After Cameroon's breakthrough performance in 1990 African appearances in the latter stages and major scalps become far more commonplace, possibly even expected. Senegal and Ghana performed admirably, but they have not come close to winning the competition. Only very recently, with Morocco in 2022, has an African team gone beyond the quarter-finals.

What if they had?

Senegal were beaten 2-0 by the 2002 tournament co-hosts Japan. Ghana were infamously denied by a Luis Suárez handball on the goal line, deliberately stopping a goalbound effort with his hand. The penalty was missed by Asamoah Gyan. Uruguay defeated Ghana in the penalty shoot-out. Both Senegal and Ghana lost at the quarter-final stage.

At the 1994 World Cup Nigeria took a youthful squad filled with future stars of the European game, but also included players with experience of European club football. Group D consisted of Argentina (with a returning Diego Maradona), Bulgaria, Greece and Nigeria. Nigeria began with an exhilarating 3-0 destruction of Bulgaria, experienced forward Rashidi Yekini powering in the opener from close range and providing an iconic, net-grasping celebration. Emmanuel Amunike's third, a diving far-post header, put a seal on the victory. Nigeria's willingness to take opponents on and attack instantly stood out. This Bulgarian side would end the tournament as legends, inspired by Hristo Stoichkov and Yordan Letchkov to reach the semi-finals. In their second group game Nigeria and Argentina stood toe to toe. Either side might have won the match but two Claudio Caniggia goals gave Argentina victory. Nigeria needed to beat Greece to progress. They would ease to a 2-0 win thanks to goals from Finidi George and Daniel Amokachi.

In the round of 16 Nigeria were drawn against a team of legends, including Paolo Maldini, Franco Baresi, Gianfranco Zola, Demetrio Albertini and Roberto Baggio. Italy would go on to the final but they slipped past Nigeria with more than a hint of fortune.

A Nigerian corner creates chaos in the Italian box. The ball pops into the air for Amunike to prod in. Italian frustration grows as they have three penalty appeals turned down. In the 76th minute Gianfranco Zola is sent off, somewhat harshly for a sliding tackle deemed to have a dangerous hooking motion. With just two minutes remaining Italy finally create a shooting opportunity inside the Nigeria penalty area. Roberto Baggio sweeps a low shot into the bottom-right corner. The game goes to extra time. Early on Nigeria create an opportunity to lead again. A precise, angled pass puts Yekini through one on one against goalkeeper Luca Marchegiani. Yekini can't quite get enough elevation on his shot and the ball bounces off Marchegiani's torso to safety. In the 100th minute Italy finally get their penalty kick. Baggio strikes home off the left-hand post. Italy defend stoutly to reach the next round.

The build-up to Baggio's equaliser involves a fortunate ricochet. Roberto Mussi creates the goal – as he dribbles, the ball bounces off a Nigerian defender, on to his left foot and back into his own path.

So what if we change the outcome of the ricochet, and the ball bounces harmlessly to safety?

Italy then have two minutes plus added time to find an equaliser. They fail. Nigeria knock Italy out of the World Cup, moving on to face Spain in the quarter-final.

Spain had emerged from Group C unbeaten but also unconvincing. They began with a 2-2 draw against

South Korea. The Koreans scored in the 85th and 90th minutes to come from two goals behind. In the next game Spain drew 1-1 with Germany, scoring from a cross that dropped into the far corner before Klinsmann equalised. Spain needed a win against Bolivia to get through to the knockout stage, winning comfortably 3-1, a Pep Guardiola penalty opening the scoring for Spain. In the knockout round the Spanish dismissed Switzerland 3-0.

In the quarter-finals Italy beat Spain 2-1, thanks to another late Baggio winner. In this version of events Nigeria have defeated Italy and are Spain's opponents. The Spanish team has significant quality, built around Barcelona and Real Madrid players. Guardiola pulls the strings from midfield while Jose Luis Enrique provides forward thrust. José Luis Caminero had a tremendous tournament in 1994, scoring two vital goals against Bolivia and striking in the quarter-final against Italy.

He opens the scoring against Nigeria, running from deep on to a beautiful forward pass by Guardiola and slipping a shot into the net. Nigeria push forward, the threat of Amokachi and Yekini causing problems for the Spanish centre-halves. Their presence inside the box draws the attention of the Spanish defenders. A cross from the Nigerian right clears the central area and Amunike arrives at the far post, much as he did in the group game against Bulgaria. His downward header sends the game into extra time. Both teams create openings but Nigeria create the crucial strike. A pass into Amokachi doesn't quite stick but the loose ball drops perfectly for Finidi George. His first touch knocks the ball past Fernando Hierro, releasing him into the Spanish penalty area. Finidi thunders a powerful right-foot strike in off the crossbar, sending Nigeria into the semi-final.

Bulgaria, Nigeria's group stage opponents, await. The Bulgarians had been inspired by Barcelona's Hristo Stoichkov to infamously dump Germany out in the quarter-final. Stoichkov curled in a beautiful free kick against Germany and he repeats the dose early on in the semi-final against Nigeria, Yordan Letchkov cleverly winning a free kick close to the Nigerian box. The magical left foot of Stoichkov flicks the ball over the wall, bending high into the top corner. 1-0 Bulgaria. The lead doesn't last long. Quick Nigerian passing results in the ball at Amokachi's feet. Having demonstrated his powerful shooting earlier in the tournament he does so once again. His first touch puts the ball through a Bulgarian defender's legs. The second fires the ball high into the Bulgarian net. Half-time with the score at 1-1.

The Nigerian manager, Clemens Westerhof, uses half-time to remind his team how they had beaten Bulgaria with ease in the group stage. They take note. Playmaker Sunday Oliseh sets Finidi George free on the right-hand side. He cuts the ball back between the six-yard box and penalty spot. Yekini arrives and blasts a finish into the bottom corner. The similarities to their opener in the group stage are remarkable. Finidi George is a creative menace out wide. Just past the hour his quick footwork sucks in two defenders, creating space to whip a cross into the box; Amokachi leaps between two Bulgarian defenders, his powerful neck muscles guiding a header firmly into the corner of the Bulgarian goal. A 3-1 lead. Stoichkov takes hold of the game, forcing Nigeria deeper and deeper towards their own goal. As his frustration mounts so too does the frequency of shots, Stoichkov shooting from all angles, but rarely hitting the target. Eventually Bulgarian pressure forces a penalty. Stoichkov fires it home to set up a tense finale, but Nigeria survive to face Brazil in a mouth-watering final.

Two years after the 1994 World Cup in the USA the Olympics would also be held there, in Atlanta. In that tournament Nigeria were the gold medallists, beating Argentina 3-2 in the final. Their semi-final opponents were Brazil. In an epic game a Nigerian squad including stars from 1994, Amokachi, Amunike and Okocha, beat Brazil 4-3. Brazil's line-up included 1994 World Cup winners Bebeto and Aldair, plus superstars Roberto Carlos, Ronaldo and Rivaldo. Nigeria showed that they had the talent to stand toe to toe with the strongest South America could offer.

Whether the 1994 final would have been a toe-to-toe affair is another question entirely. Brazil in 1994 were a pragmatic team, reliant upon the attacking skills of Romario and Bebeto, while being defensively solid. In the final Brazil and Italy played out a dull 0-0 draw that

Brazil won on penalties. Earlier in the tournament Brazil were also involved in a thrilling 3-2 victory against the Netherlands. The difference between the two games was that the Dutch attacked Brazil, leaving the Brazilians space to counter-attack. This would likely be the case in a final against Nigeria.

Brazil concede far more possession initially than anyone anticipated, the wonderful deep-lying playmaking skills of Sunday Oliseh dictating the tempo of the game. Oliseh's abilities would earn him moves to Juventus and Borussia Dortmund later in his career. Oliseh also possessed the ability to strike from distance, best evidenced in the stunning half-volley he scored against Spain at the 1998 World Cup. He opens the scoring in the final, his probing and influence pushing Brazil back to the edge of their own box. Finidi receives the ball wide, dribbling at the full-back before releasing the pass infield. Dunga has dropped too deep in his defensive midfield position, allowing Oliseh the space to touch the ball out of his feet and strike a low, cutting shot into the bottom corner down by the near post.

Brazil learn from the opening goal, closing down the Nigerian midfield. Oliseh struggles to break the defensive lines as Dunga and Mauro Silva have closed the gaps. On one attempt to play in Amokachi the passing lane is not wide enough. Mauro Silva stretches to cut out the pass. Dunga picks up the loose ball, quickly playing a short pass into Mazinho. Mazinho strikes an early pass behind the

Nigerian defence for Romario to sprint on to. The master of the toe-poke finish prods past Peter Rufai to equalise.

The game goes quiet into half-time. Brazil have far more possession in the second half but Nigeria are not pushing forward as much. There is no real space for Brazil to counter-attack and Nigeria are unable to break through the Brazilian defence. Both sides toiling in the heat, the game looks set for extra time approaching the final ten minutes.

Coach Westerhof decides he doesn't want extra time. He wants to try to win the game. From the bench he brings on Nigeria's great magician, Jay-Jay Okocha. Okocha's mesmerising dribbling skills drew admiration from football fans around the world. He spent one season at PSG, playing alongside Ronaldinho. The two spurred each other on to ever more entertaining heights. Okocha's wonderful tricks create chaos in the Brazilian defence, twisting and turning them inside and out. With mere moments left on the clock Okocha dances past Aldair and Branco into a gap that didn't seem to exist. The penalty box opens up and Okocha bobbles a pass towards the penalty spot. Yekini strides on to the pass and the bobbling ball pops up perfectly for a smoothly timed half-volley to crash in off the crossbar, down on to the line and up into the roof of the net. Nigerian celebrations run wild. The game is won. All that is left is for captain Stephen Keshi to lift the gold trophy in the glorious green of the Nigerian Super Eagles.

Not only would winning the World Cup be phenomenal for African football, it would have a deep impact on European football. Players would have been more attracted to playing for their home nation, the nation of their birth or the nation of their parents. A generation or generations of African players might have chosen to play for someone other than the name associated with them in the history books.

For certain the history of French football changes.

In August 1994 a young midfielder comes off the bench for France against the Czech Republic. France are two goals behind but this young man manages to find two goals and erase the deficit. This young man could have chosen to play for Algeria but he chose France. This man is Zinedine Zidane.

If Zidane sees an African nation win the World Cup in 1994 and chooses to play for Algeria, do France win the 1998 World Cup or the 2000 Euros? Just removing Zidane creates questions about those successes.

What if Patrick Vieira chose to play for Senegal?

At the 2002 World Cup Senegal reach the quarter-final stages. In the opening game they beat France 1-0, defeating the reigning champions just as Cameroon did in 1990.

Their central midfield is Aliou Cisse, Salif Diao and Papa Bouba Diop, all three very fine footballers but none of them as forceful and gifted as Vieira. They were knocked out by Turkey in the quarter-finals. Surely with Vieira in the team the case for them going at least one round further is a strong one.

The impact of African players choosing to play for France has deepened in the decades since the 1998 French World Cup win. If Nigeria are champions in 1994 and France do not win in 1998 and 2000 a swathe of players choose different nations. The World Cup-winning squad of 2018 is shredded as we can see from the table below.

Kylian Mbappe	Algeria or Cameroon
Paul Pogba	Guinea
Samuel Umtiti	Cameroon
Steve Mandanda	Democratic Republic of Congo
Blaise Matuidi	Angola or Congo
N'Golo Kante	Mali
Ousmane Dembele	Mali
Benjamin Mendy	Congo
Djibril Sidibe	Congo
Presnel Kimpembe	Congo
Nabil Fekir	Algeria
Adil Rami	Morocco

The African nations are strengthened, and France significantly weakened. If Mbappé chooses Cameroon their ranks are bolstered significantly, while Democratic Republic of Congo gain a whole new defence and goalkeeper.

If Nigeria had been able to hold on to that lead against Italy the landscape of global football is changed forever, becoming far less Eurocentric, with Africa a powerhouse the equal of South America. All because of one bounce of a football.

WHAT IF HUNGARY 1954
PLAYED HOLLAND 1974?

Influence and impact do not guarantee victory.

Two of the most influential teams in the history of football both blew their big chance. Twenty years apart, Hungary and the Netherlands were the dominant teams at a World Cup. Twenty years apart they both lost in the final against West Germany.

It would not be the performances of West Germany that inspired generations to come. It would be the tales of the greatest runners-up.

The Hungarian 'Golden Team' came together at the end of the 1940s. From 1950 until 1956 the team lost just one game.

That game happened to be the World Cup Final. They went to the 1952 Olympic Games after two years unbeaten but Ferenc Puskás would later say that it was only at the Helsinki Games that their football would really start to flow. Hungary beat Romania 2-1 in the preliminary round but then crushed Italy 3-0, Turkey 7-1 and Sweden 6-0 to reach the final. In the gold medal match Hungary beat Yugoslavia 2-0.

The core of the team at the 1952 Olympics would remain together until 1956, only breaking up after the 1956 Hungarian Revolution. The players flocked away from the country to play abroad, many of them even earning international caps for their new homes.

Puskás was the most famous player, the inspirational leader and goalscorer. Sándorr Kocsis, Nándor Hidegkuti, Zoltán Czibor, József Bozsik and Gyula Grosics were the spine of a team managed by Gusztáv Sebes.

Sebes was born in 1906, a child of the Austro-Hungarian Empire. This was an important factor as the dissemination of culture led to the sharing of ideas. Hungary's 'Golden Team' did not emerge from nowhere, but was the product of footballing ideas merging. Following World War Two the Hungarian government became involved in football, aiming to make the Hungarian team a symbol of greatness and of their ideology. Communism was at its peak and Sebes fitted the bill. A former trade union leader who once stated that 'the bitter struggle between capitalism and communism is fought not only between our societies, but also on the pitch', he was clearly the perfect man to lead the team.

The Hungarian style of play was greatly influenced by Viennese café culture. The café was seen as the place for intellectuals to share ideas and those involved in football were no different. The strength of links between Hungary and Austria allowed those ideas to pass freely.

The style of the Hungarian team had two key influences: the Austrian side of the 1930s and the Englishman Jimmy Hogan. Sebes stated that Hungary 'played football the way Jimmy Hogan taught us'. Hogan spent time in Austria, Hungary and the Netherlands in the 1910s and 20s as both a player and coach. Hogan believed in a passing-and-possession-based style, a whirl of movement. He worked with both Sebes and Rinus Michels, influencing both the Hungarian style of 1954 and the Dutch of 1974.

The Austrian *Wunderteam* of the 1930s was led by Hugo Meisl. Meisl had created another team with swirling and whirling interchangeable positions. The key for them was the forward Matthias Sindelar, who would drop deep to create midfield overloads and space for players to run forward. Meisl died in 1937. His death, plus the outbreak of the Second World War, prevented the *Wunderteam* from reaching its full potential, but its legacy was an influence on the Hungarian team of the 50s. Austria and Hungary provided the blueprints for Dutch total football, the biggest influence on world football today.

The Hungarians used a 3-2-3-2 formation with a withdrawn centre-forward. Hidegkuti dropped deep, Puskás and Kocsis filled the space. Bozsik stepped out of the back line to act as a playmaker. The full-backs were required to step forward and support the wingers, thus Hungary asked defenders to also be attackers, a manner of playing that would be considered in keeping with modern football. The Hungarians made use of triangles, one-twos and third-man runs. Former England manager Ron Greenwood described the Hungarians as using 'moving triangles' and rapid combinations. Tiki-taka before the term had even been coined.

By 1954 Hungary went into the World Cup as favourites. The group stage was a concept now alien to us, with two teams seeded and two unseeded. The seeded teams did not have to play the unseeded teams. West Germany and South Korea were the unseeded teams in the group. Hungary defeated Korea 9-0 and West Germany 8-3. Hungary then faced South American opponents, beating both Brazil and Uruguay, the finalists from 1950, by the same score of 4-2. Puskás was injured in the win against Germany and missed the quarter- and semi-final. He would return for the final.

The final against West Germany was sodden, played out on a quagmire of a pitch. Hungary went two goals ahead inside ten minutes, scored by Puskás and Czibor. West Germany scored two to equalise through Morlock and Rahn but Hungary pounded Germany, with the woodwork being struck, efforts cleared off the line, and then a stunning point-blank save by West German goalkeeper Turek from a powerful volley. Puskás missed a great chance in the 47th minute.

The game starts to resemble pinball inside the West German penalty box. A Kocsis header hit the bar. Puskás misses another great chance in the 67th, striking the foot of Turek. Hidegkuti hits the side netting with Turek stranded in the 78th minute. In the 84th Rahn scores his second, low and hard from the edge of the box into the bottom left corner. Germany led 3-2. Two minutes later Hungary have a goal disallowed. Germany hold on and the best team of the 1954 tournament finish second.

By 1974 the Netherlands' status as a global powerhouse had become well established. It was a long, hard road for Dutch football. The national team featured in both the 1934 and 1938 tournaments, losing in the first knockout rounds. It was not until Dutch domestic football started to have an impact on the European stage that the national team began to rise to prominence.

It was Feyenoord who initially led the way in the 1960s. Ajax receive most of the attention, but it should not be forgotten that Feyenoord won the European Cup in 1969/70, then followed it up with a UEFA Cup win 1973/74. It was Feyenoord who supplied more players in 1974 (seven) but it was Ajax (six) who supplied the bigger stars. It should be noted that one Ajax player had registered for Barcelona just before the tournament having signed from Ajax. Johan Cruyff.

The Feyenoord team of the 1970s was managed by an Austrian, Ernst Happel. The lineage is quite apparent. Happel played for Austria Vienna in the 1940s through to 1959, with a brief spell in Paris breaking this up. Their star players were Wim Jansen and Willem van Hanegem, who would be key players for the national team in their midfield roles.

This team emerged at the same time as the legendary Ajax team. Unsurprisingly a fierce competitive rivalry emerged that burns through to this day. Ajax were influenced by the methods of Englishman Vic Buckingham who managed the club twice, the second time immediately before Rinus Michels took over in 1965. It was Michels' team who made Europe stand up and take notice of total football. Ajax won a trio of European Cups from 1971–73, immediately after Feyenoord's victory, making it four in a row for the Dutch. Rinus Michels won the first of the Ajax trophies. Romanian coach Ştefan Kovács won the next two, but Ajax still played the total football style.

While Europe had become quite familiar with this style of play, the world would become aware of it at the 1974 finals. Ajax played a hybrid 4-3-3/3-4-3 formation. Their actual formation is often disputed due to the fluidity of the player movements and a central defender stepping out from defence into midfield. The full-backs could operate as central defenders, tucking inside if needed or pushing up. The trio of midfielders and forwards rotated with regularity, creating fluid attacking patterns. The Dutch also counter-pressed aggressively, swarming the player in possession and rushing opponents into errors. This was a prototype version, without the later sophistication of cutting out passing lines or targeting individuals. Total football simply swarmed.

Ajax players formed the core of the 1974 team. Suurbier, Haan, Krol, Neeskens and Rep all started the final as did ex-Ajax star Johan Cruyff. Feyenoord players Rijsbergen, Jansen and van Hanegem also started the final.

The Dutch sent shock waves through world football with their performances in 1974. They had not even appeared in any finals since 1938. They went through qualification unbeaten for the 1974 tournament before being drawn in a group with Sweden, Bulgaria and Uruguay. The first game was a 2-0 win against Uruguay. After a 0-0 draw with Sweden the Dutch thumped Bulgaria 4-1 to confirm their place in the second round. There was little of significance in the 0-0 with Sweden, bar Johan Cruyff amazing the world with his now famous turn. This was an era of two group stages and in the second group the Netherlands were drawn with East Germany, Argentina and Brazil.

In the first game of the second group the Netherlands thrashed Argentina 4-0. A comfortable 2-0 win was followed by an equally comfortable 2-0 victory against the defending world champions, Brazil. At this point the stories of Hungary and the Netherlands converge. Twenty years apart the tale of the best team of the tournament is repeated. As with 1954 the Netherlands faced West Germany. As with 1954 the team of the tournament take an early lead. As with 1954 it is West Germany who end up holding the trophy aloft.

From the kick-off the Dutch work possession, stringing together a lengthy passing move that finds Cruyff outside the West German box. He dribbles into the area and is brought down. A penalty after barely a minute of the final. Johan Neeskens hammers the spot kick down the centre for the early lead. After 25 minutes the West Germans have a penalty of their own, tucked in by Paul Breitner. Minutes before half-time Gerd Müller completes the turnaround, 2-1 to West Germany. In the second half the West Germans are under intense pressure, Sepp Maier making several saves and the Netherlands missing a number of good chances. West Germany hold on to thwart total football. To add to the pain, in 1978, the Netherlands would reach the final again, losing 3-1 to Argentina as the candle of the first total football era went out.

What if the two most influential teams of their eras faced off? Would we get a feast of attacking football?

When we have fantasy match-ups the temptation is to expect that the attacking talents on show would dominate, relegating the defenders to the supporting cast. This is because we all want to be entertained and wowed. Most people have a healthy respect for high-class defending but it is the play of forwards that leaves you breathless. There is a reason that the majority of fantasy football match-ups don't throw out 'what if Italian Catenaccio faced the Swiss Verrou?' For the sake of entertainment and the anticipated thrill ride we will side with the forwards.

The match should be played in conditions that fit the two teams. Rules will be recognisable and realistic to both. The goalkeepers will be allowed to pick up back passes, players will not be allowed in the penalty area at goal kicks and there will be no substitutes. By 1974 substitutes were allowed, but the majority of the Dutch players would have played in matches where no substitutions were allowed, while the Hungarians would not have played competitive games with substitutes. No substitutions will be permitted in this match-up. The choice of ball is important. The super heavy ball of 1954 would be unfair to the Dutch and too big an advantage for the Hungarians. The only ball that would be a compromise would be the iconic 1970 World Cup ball, the 32-panel, black-and-white Telstar.

The stadium should also be appropriate for the teams. A vast European concrete bowl of the era would fit perfectly. Especially if it has been used for an Olympic Games previously. Spectators smear across the stands in a sea of deep red and brilliant orange. The officials are clad in all black, with just watches, whistles and flags. No technology on show here. Cruyff and Puskás come together to toss the specially commissioned coin.

The Hungarians kick off. The Dutch are primed like sprinters. Puskás taps the ball to Kocsis, who plays back to Bozsik. A stampede of orange charges towards Bozsik. Under heavy pressure he loses composure and smashes the ball out of play. The Netherlands are going to press with fury.

Early Dutch energy is too much for the Magyars. Rep, Neeskens and Cruyff swamp Buzansky. The ball breaks loose and Rep pokes a pass to the supporting Jansen. He rolls square to Van Hanegem. Jansen's pass has allowed enough time for the pressers to disperse into space. Van Hanegem picks out Cruyff's run. One touch carries him into the left side of the penalty area. Rep is square and Cruyff picks him out. Rep thumps a first-time half-volley into the roof of the net. The Netherlands lead 1-0.

Another press from Rensenbrink and Rep causes Bozsik to rush, clearing straight to Krol. Krol finds Neeskens in the centre of the pitch. Neeskens combines with Cruyff before passing wide to Rep on the right. Rep slows the play down, then swings a cross to the far post. Rensenbrink's header loops wide of the post.

The Hungarians are struggling with the game barely ten minutes old.

Hidegkuti, famous for dropping out of the centre-forward position to receive the ball, decides to take over. He drops from an advanced midfield position to the point where he is alongside Zakarias in central midfield. This allows Bozsik to also drop deeper, almost forming a back four. The Dutch press is less effective with Bozsik able to play simple passes into Hidegkuti before the sprinting press can come.

The Dutch press aims to swamp the man in possession rather than block lines to play forward. Hidegkuti is able to receive and play to Czibor or Toth wide with ease. Hungary begin to get a grip on the game and Dutch energy starts to drop. The press is a little slower, a little less sharp, a little less fierce.

Hidegkuti receives in space centrally, the Dutch press having been bypassed. Instead of playing the forward pass he dribbles. Van Hanegem is beaten by a change of pace. Hidegkuti advances towards the Dutch area. Haan and Rijsbergen sense the threat and step towards the dribbler from their central defensive positions, which creates space for Puskás and Kocsis. Hidegkuti slots a pass for Puskás. Left foot cocked to release a thunderbolt, he instead strokes a pass into the path of Kocsis. A low finish tucked into the bottom corner by Kocsis levels at 1-1.

Midway through the half and two teams who enjoy passing the ball in short patterns appear to be allowing each other to paint pretty but harmless pictures. Fast, short passes go nowhere against a wall of opposing players.

Cruyff decides to inject some energy into a Dutch attack, receiving and jinking between two Hungarian defenders. His shot from 20 yards skims low and wide. The Hungarians are awakened. Bozsik and Zakarias play a quick one-two in midfield. Hidegkuti receives a pass infield. He slots a ball between Rijsbergen and Suurbier for Czibor. Czibor reaches the pass yards in front of the touchline and lifts a cross to the six-yard box. Kocsis gets to the ball just before the fists of Jongbloed to head Hungary into the lead.

The Netherlands look furious. The energy has returned to their press. Cruyff seems to be putting all of his soul into pressing Hidegkuti. The first time Cruyff gets tight he doesn't get the timing right. Hidegkuti skips away from Johan and is only halted by Wim Jansen's foul. On the second occasion Cruyff times the pressure perfectly and picks Hidegkuti's pocket. Cruyff's pass puts Rep in behind the defence, one on one with Grosics. Rep strikes low and hard but the shot clatters off the ankles of the Hungarian goalkeeper and away to safety.

Half-time is just moments away. Cruyff gets on the ball once again. He passes to Jansen and instantly runs forward. Jansen lets the ball run to Van Hanegem, who has seen Cruyff's run. The lifted pass is perfect for Cruyff but it also looks to be perfect for Grosics. Dutchman, Hungarian and ball arrive in the same patch of space at the same moment. The Dutchman flicks the ball over the Hungarian, stays on his feet, then strokes the ball into a now unguarded net. A magnificent goal to take the game into half-time at 2-2.

The Dutch start with the press, just as they did in the first half. Hungary are ready for the squeeze this time and Hidegkuti drops into the deeper position immediately. Bozsik, Hidegkuti and Zakarias move the ball at high speed, bypassing the Dutchmen. There are no early errors in the second half and no real adventure in possession. That is until Ruud Krol, scorer of goals from distance against Argentina, Italy and West Germany, dribbles forward from defence to strike a rocket. Grosics reacts superbly to tip the shot over the crossbar.

Krol's adventure brings the match back into sparkling life. The passing and movement of Hungary is bright and rhythmical, the moving triangles keeping the Dutch defence on edge. Haan and Rijsbergen block goal attempts from Kocsis and Hidegkuti. Puskás receives a pass 25 yards from the Dutch goal. The defence hesitates, leaving

Puskás the space to shoot. His famously powerful left foot belts an effort low at goal. Jongbloed dives low to his left. He gets two hands to the shot but his wrists are weak, and rather than deflecting the strike wide of the post the Dutch custodian merely shovels the ball into the corner of the net. The Magyars have the lead.

The Hungarians see an opportunity to wear down the Dutch. Toth dribbles against Suurbier, generating enough space to cross. Czibor attacks the ball at the far post but his header is wide of a relieved Jongbloed's goal.

Time is running out for the Dutch. Cruyff knows he has to change the flow of the game. Taking a leaf out of Hidegkuti's book Cruyff drops in alongside his central defenders to receive the ball. He drives forward. Surging beyond Bozsik and Zakarias, drawing Lorant towards him. Rensenbrink and Rep occupy Lantos and Buzansky. This means that Rep is completely free. Cruyff slots him in with a low pass. Rep is now one on one with Grosics, who advances rapidly. Rep flicks the ball over Grosics but a recovering Lorant hacks the effort away before it can cross the line.

At the other end a fine Kocsis dribble threatens the Dutch defence. Haan clips his ankles and brings Kocsis down. Hidegkuti lines up the free kick. At Wembley in 1953 Hidegkuti netted a free kick that helped send England into freefall. Here he dips the shot over the wall but straight at Jongbloed. What should be a simple save is fumbled but the Dutch goalkeeper pounces on the ball before a sniffing Kocsis can get there. Jongbloed looks like he is still a little shaken from the Puskás goal.

With just five minutes remaining Czibor receives a pass and spins his marker. He rolls a gentle pass into the path of Kocsis. Kocsis steps on the ball and pulls it backwards away from the defender, creating time and space for himself. This also allows the Netherlands defence to gather, and once Kocsis' pass has reached the feet of Bozsik ten orange shirts are between him and the goal. Yet Bozsik picks out a brilliant pass, eliminating four Dutchmen and finding Puskás on the edge of the penalty area. Puskás controls quickly then cracks another fearsome left-foot shot towards the near top corner from the right edge of the area. Jongbloed doesn't move – whether he thinks the shot is going wide or he has given up is impossible to tell – but the strike catches the netting. Hungary celebrate a fourth goal.

The Netherlands do not give up. In the 1978 World Cup Final they faced the hosting Argentines in the final, losing 3-1 in extra time but hit the post at the very end of 90 minutes. Rob Rensenbrink, who came so close in 1978, does the same here. A Cruyff shot cannons around in the Hungarian area. Rensenbrink gets a snap shot away and off the base of the post, Grosics' left hand well beaten. As the ball trundles out of play the referee blows his whistle. The Dutch, most unfortunate of runners-up, have missed out again. The 'Mighty Magyars' narrowly edge through and show why they are so admired and influential.

WHAT IF THE REF HAD CALLED IT RIGHT?

The Hand of God

The first 50 minutes of the 1986 World Cup quarter-final between Argentina and England had been tight, close-fought and engrossing. The attacking talents of both sides had been nullified. But Argentina had a genius in their side.

Diego Maradona sets off on a run, strolls past Hoddle, shimmies past Reid and goes to play a one-two. The ball spins off the outstretched boot of England midfielder Steve Hodge and loops up towards the penalty spot. Maradona beats the England keeper Peter Shilton to the ball and gives Argentina the lead. The England players protest, chasing the referee back to the halfway line, vigorously pointing at their hands. Replays clearly show that the ball was punched into the England goal. Maradona insists *he* did not handle the ball. It was the 'Hand of God' that scored.

If the officials had disallowed the goal would England have gone on to win the game or even the tournament? Five minutes later Maradona scores the goal of the World

Cup, and arguably any World Cup, when he slaloms past half the England team with a mesmerising dribble and slots past Shilton. The prospect of Maradona inspiring an Argentinian win was always likely, but England had every right to feel aggrieved. Had Bobby Robson's team progressed, there is a decent chance they would have beaten Belgium in the semi-final, but it's tough to call an England win against West Germany in the final. What is for certain if the referee calls it right, football would have been denied one of its most iconic images and one of its seminal moments. Would Maradona be remembered more fondly had he owned up, played fair? Not in Argentina, for sure.

The Schumacher 'Assault'

The definition of a dangerous challenge, and of a late challenge, has evolved through the football decades. It is difficult to deny that one of the all-time worst offences was seen in the 1982 World Cup semi-final between West Germany and France.

With the game poised at 1-1 in the second half, Michel Platini chips a beautiful through ball that splits the West German defence. Patrick Battiston is favourite to win the ball as the West German right-back Manni Kaltz rushes across to cover. As Battiston steers the ball towards goal from just outside the penalty area the West German goalkeeper Schumacher is level with the penalty spot. The camera follows the ball as it bounces agonisingly past the post. When the camera pans back, Battiston is prone on the floor. Within seconds the French players are gesturing wildly for the stretcher. Battiston never moves. People in the crowd and watching on TV around the world are thinking the very worst. Schumacher looks on unconcerned.

The replay shows that Schumacher hits Battiston in the head with the full force of his body while leading with his elbow. He is so late for the ball it would be easy to argue that connecting with it was never the goalkeeper's intention. The referee does not even issue a card. Thankfully, Battiston recovers. Yet even with the more physical nature of the game in the 1980s, Schumacher has to be sent off. If he is, it is unlikely we witness the thrilling 3-3 draw that ensued with West Germany going through to the semi-finals on penalties. The likelihood is that the thrilling French team of Platini, Six, Giresse and Rocheteau would have proved too much for ten men. Would they have beaten a rampant, Rossi-inspired Italy in the final? Many would have loved the chance to find out.

The Lampard Ghost Goal

England versus Germany in the World Cup. A shot hits the underside of the bar and bounces down. Was it over the line? Pandemonium ensues as the players surround the referee. No, this is not 1966, this is 2010.

England are facing Germany in the round of the last 16 due to turgid draws at the group stage with Algeria and the USA. A win in either game would have seen them play Ghana. England manager Fabio Capello is already under fire with his team selection as he tries to solve the perennial problem of whether Lampard and Gerrard can play together in the centre of midfield. Lampard starts alongside Barry. Gerrard starts on the left wing.

The Germans are strong, slick and incisive and are two goals up after half an hour. But England pull a goal back through the most surprising of goalscorers, centre-half Upson. It is now a different game. Minutes later Defoe turns on the edge of the German box, the ball breaks to Lampard who lofts the ball over the German goalkeeper Neuer and against the bar. When the ball bounces down it lands at least a yard over the goal line. The kind of distance that reduces any doubt. And yet, the officials do not see it.

So, what if the referee makes the right call and awards England the goal? From two goals down to two-all is a big psychological swing at any level. With England chasing the game in the second half, the Germans score two on the break through Müller to make the game look one-sided, yet for long periods it was anything but. This was the last real chance for England's golden generation at a World Cup and they could be rightly frustrated at their elimination. They would have run into peak Spain later in the tournament had they progressed, so it's very unlikely they would have lifted the trophy. What Lampard's 'goal' did do, was hasten the acceptance of goal-line technology, which was in place within two years and is widely acknowledged as a huge improvement for football.

The De Jong World Cup Final Foul

There can be no greater accolade for a referee than to officiate in the World Cup Final itself. It follows that there can be no worse occasion on which to make a bad decision. The one game when the eyes of the world are watching. The fate of the bad decision fell to English referee Howard Webb in the World Cup Final of 2010 between Holland and Spain.

The former Rotherham policeman was one of the most respected officials in the game, and most people thought he thoroughly deserved the crowning moment of his career. Fans and connoisseurs alike were looking forward to the match which featured two of the more technically accomplished, tactically aware teams in world football. Of course, all that meant was that the first 20 minutes were error-strewn and full of niggly fouls. Both teams were looking to gain control. The Dutch defence make a headed clearance which falls to Xavi, who cushion volleys the ball across the pitch towards Alonso. Van Bommel closes in on Alonso who wins the header. Then, in steams De Jong, foot chin-high, and poleaxes the Spanish midfielder. It's a straight red.

Webb explains later that he has missed the point of contact as his view is obstructed by Van Bommel and Alonso. What is mystifying, with all the officials wearing microphones, is that none of his assistants spoke to him. De Jong says he pleaded it was accidental. 'Don't make such a big decision so early in the game.' In any major final there is always added pressure on the officials to 'not spoil' the occasion for the watching audience of many millions. Luckily for Webb, Spain went on to win the final in extra time by a solitary goal from Iniesta. If he had called it right and sent off De Jong, Spain would surely have passed the ten men of Holland off the pitch and won in normal time. No change to the outcome, but a moment that has lived with Webb ever since.

The Henry Handball

European qualification for the 2010 World Cup saw 53 teams competing for 13 places in nine groups. The top nine teams went straight through to the finals, with the best eight runners-up playing off over two legs. France had surprisingly finished second to Serbia in Group 7 and were up against the Republic of Ireland who finished behind Italy in Group 8. France won the first leg in Ireland 1-0 and seemed on course for the finals. The indefatigable Irish had other ideas.

France started confidently in the stadium where they had won the World Cup in 1998. Slowly, but surely, the Irish came into the game, and it was no great surprise when Robbie Keane fired past Lloris just before half-time. In the second half there were chances at both ends but no further goals and the game went into extra time. In the

What if Cantona doesn't retire? Do United win the treble?

What if Celtic and Rangers had joined the Premier League? Would they have dominated like they have in Scotland?

What if Messi and Ronaldo had been team-mates instead of rivals?

What if Tom Finney had been born in a different era? How many trophies might England have won?

What if Guardiola coached in League Two? Chequebook manager or visionary?

What if Pele had played in Europe? Would his legacy have been even greater?

What if England had built a team around Glenn Hoddle? Why did so many managers fail to trust his talent?

What if English clubs had not been banned from Europe after Heysel? Which teams lost out the most?

What if Gerrard had signed for Chelsea? Would he and Lampard have worked in central midfield?

What if Brian Clough had managed England? Would he have been successful at international level?

What if Ajax had never sold their best players? Would they now have the most European titles?

What if the Munich Air Crash had not happened? Who would have been England's captain in 1966?

What if an African team won the World Cup? How would it impact on European national teams?

What if Gazza had scored in the 1996 European Championships semi-final? Would England teams have been more successful since?

What if Michael Owen had stayed fit? How many medals did he miss out on?

What if Jimmy Greaves had not been injured during the 1966 World Cup? Would England have had a different goalscoring hero?

first period the French were convinced they should have had a penalty when Given appeared to bring down Anelka. Their frustration, however, was nothing compared to that suffered by the Irish.

With just seven minutes of extra time left Malouda launches a free kick into the Irish penalty area. It clears the Irish defence and bounces towards the far post where Henry is lurking. He touches the ball with his hand not once, but twice, first to stop the ball going out of play, then to control it so he can flick the ball to Gallas, who scores. After being chased by the Irish players, Swedish referee Martin Anderson indicates that the ball had hit Henry on the body. After the delirious celebrations, Henry stands in the centre circle smiling.

So what if the referee calls it right? The goal is disallowed and the game would probably have gone to penalties, where Ireland would have had every chance of going through to South Africa. Had they done so they would have found themselves in a group with Uruguay, Mexico and the hosts. Some kind of justice was seen when France performed abysmally and finished bottom of the four teams. It's not difficult to see the Irish making it through the group, and although they would probably have gone out to Argentina in the round of 16, the World Cup would have been enhanced not only by the presence of the team, but by the all-singing, all-dancing Irish fans.

The Van Persie Sending-Off

Playing against peak 2011 Barcelona would have been difficult for any team from any era. Playing against peak Barcelona with ten men was nigh-on impossible, as Arsenal found out to their cost in the Champions League round of 16.

The Gunners held a one-goal advantage from the first leg. Arsène Wenger's team had more than held their own and had played with belief and confidence. The second leg was in the cauldron that is the Nou Camp. Once again Arsenal went toe to toe with Barcelona and were certainly not intimidated either by the atmosphere, nor by the supreme skill of the opposition. It took a moment of magic from Messi, inevitably, just before half-time for Barcelona to make the score 1-1 on aggregate. Even so, Arsenal were not finished. Just eight minutes into the second half Nasri swings in a corner and in the confusion Busquets heads into his own net. Arsenal not only lead over the two legs, they have an all-important away goal. Three minutes later Cesc Fàbregas plays a through ball to Robin van Persie, who takes it in his stride but shoots wide. Van Persie has been flagged offside. The Swiss referee Massimo Busacca has blown his whistle a second before Van Persie shoots. He then books the Arsenal striker on the grounds that he 'kicked the ball away' and sends him off for a second yellow. An incredible call. Ten-man Arsenal hang on for 15 minutes, but then two goals in quick succession from Xavi and Messi put Barcelona through.

So, what if the referee had found a less draconian interpretation to the letter of the law? Arsenal were very well placed in the tie. Had they scored again it would have been over, and there was every chance they could have. Van Persie was without doubt one of the best strikers in the world at the time. Of course, Barcelona might well have produced their brilliant best and scored the two goals they needed even with Van Persie on the pitch. Yet with Arsenal's confidence growing it would have taken something special. Barcelona went on to beat José Mourinho's Real Madrid in the semi-final, and Manchester United at Wembley. For all their magnificent effort over the two legs against Barcelona it is hard to see Arsenal lifting the Champions League trophy. With Barcelona out of the tournament Manchester United could have done though. The biggest loser of Massimo Busacca's decision might well have been Sir Alex Ferguson.

The Tony Brown 'Offside' Goal

For English football fans of a certain age, there is one referee's decision that stands out among all referees' decisions. It occurred in 1971 at Elland Road as Leeds were taking on West Bromwich Albion.

As ever, Leeds were going for the First Division title, but West Brom had some decent players including England international Jeff Astle and Tony Brown, who would go on to be the top scorer that year with 28 goals. It was Brown who had opened the scoring after a mistake by

Jack Charlton and although Leeds dominated the game, Albion had more than one easy chance to add to their lead. Then came the moment that would see referee Colin Tinkler hit the headlines.

Time is ebbing away as Norman Hunter brings the ball out of defence and attempts a pass to Johnny Giles. It is intercepted by Tony Brown, who dribbles forward to see Colin Suggett five yards offside. The linesman flags, Brown hesitates, but Mr Tinkler waves play on. Brown runs clean through towards goalkeeper Sprake in the Leeds goal, before passing to the supporting Astle, who scores into an empty net. This is the 1970s. Within seconds there are more fans and policemen on the pitch than players. It takes minutes to clear. The goal stands. Although Leeds pull a goal back with two minutes to play, they lose 2-1.

So, what if Mr Tinkler had made the right call? The offside law was very straightforward in those days. There had been no amendments about interfering with play, or second phase and the like. By the laws as they were played then, Colin Suggett wasn't just offside, he was 'miles' offside. This decision had a profound effect on the season as Leeds lost out on winning the Division One title by just one point in what was Arsenal's double-winning year. Leeds would have continued their quest for the European Cup the following season, which saw Arsenal knocked out in the quarter-finals by the brilliant Dutch side Ajax. Would Leeds have fared any better? The odds are they would have done. That year they won the Inter-Cities Fairs Cup, beating Juventus in the final. Ajax against Leeds would have been a match to savour.

Ferguson header v Villarreal

By the strict letter of the law, there are very few corner kicks where the physical wrestling that goes on could not result in a free kick to the defending team or a penalty to the attacking side. It is the inconsistency in applying the laws of the game by referees that has fans in uproar.

On 24 August 2005 Villarreal were playing Everton in a Champions League third qualifying round match. The Spanish team had won the first leg at Goodison Park 2-1 and were well set to go through when they took the lead early in the second leg. David Moyes' team had other ideas. They dug in, and midway through the second half Mikel Arteta scored a wonderful free kick to put the tie in the balance.

Minutes later Arteta swings in a superb corner. Everton talisman Duncan Ferguson leaps high and powers in a header, only for it to be disallowed by the referee. That referee was probably the most famous official in the world at the time Pierluigi Collina. What is for certain is that there is no infringement by Ferguson. And even with the luxury of frame-by-frame replays, it is very difficult to see any offence by any Everton player at all. Of course, with minutes to go, Villarreal hit Everton on the break and score to go through 4-2 on aggregate.

To break into the top four of the Premier League had been a monumental effort by Everton. To draw Villarreal was unlucky in itself, given that the Spanish side went on to reach the semi-finals that year where they lost to Arsenal. Collina's decision had a huge impact on Everton's season. Mentally the side were clearly shattered by their Champions League exit. Immediately after they lost six games on the run without scoring a goal and were bottom of the Premier League. Eventually they recovered to 11th but their chances of repeating their top-four finish were long gone. But what if Everton had finished in the top four with the momentum and confidence from a Champions League run? What if Dimitar Berbatov had signed for Everton instead of Spurs on the promise of another shot at the Champions League, or Nicholas Anelka had chosen the Toffees instead of Bolton? One decision on the field can have a massive effect off it.

Collina announced his retirement almost immediately after the game. Duncan Ferguson announced his retirement at the end of the season. Everton have never since qualified for the Champions League.

The Sol Campbell Winning Goals

If having a winning goal disallowed in the last few minutes of a major tournament is unlucky, what if it happens twice? Step forward Sol Campbell.

The first time occurred in the epic 1998 round of 16 game between England and Argentina. The game that seemed to have everything. Michael Owen's brilliant solo, a superb training ground routine for Zanetti to make it 2-2, and David Beckham sent off just after half-time. Ten-man England battled magnificently in the second half. With ten minutes to go Darren Anderton swings in a corner. Alan Shearer jumps with the Argentinian keeper Roa but it is Campbell, standing just behind them, who heads home. To disallow the goal for a push on the keeper is harsh in the extreme.

The second time occurred in 2004 in the European Championship quarter-final against Portugal. Michael Owen had opened the scoring early on for England. Helder Postiga had equalised very late for Portugal. Then, in the last minute, Beckham swings in a free kick and Campbell heads against the bar. The ball rebounds back and Campbell beats both John Terry and the Portuguese keeper Ricardo to head in what is certainly the winner. Except it isn't. Yet again the referee disallows the goal for a push on the keeper, which again is harsh in the extreme.

So what if the referee had called it for England? What is most galling for Campbell is that with both goals it was a team-mate who was accused of fouling the keeper. In both cases there is very little contact. Frustration and disbelief are etched on Campbell's face each time. In 1998 England would have had Holland, Brazil and the brilliant hosts France in the way of lifting the World Cup. Even England optimists would be hard pressed to make a case. In 2004 it is different. If Campbell's header stands,

England play Holland in the semi-final and then Greece in the European Championship Final. There is every chance the golden generation would have lived up to their name and lifted England's first major trophy for 38 years.

WHAT IF PAUL GASCOIGNE HAD SCORED IN THE EURO 96 SEMI-FINAL?

Euro 96 has been romanticised to the point where it has become difficult to distinguish the real events from the myth. What is for sure is that England produced a spellbinding demolition of the Dutch, a redemptive penalty shoot-out victory against Spain and went toe to toe with Germany in the semi-final, until the spectre of penalties returned.

England's tournament began with a net-busting strike from Alan Shearer against Switzerland, but a drab match finished 1-1 following a late Swiss penalty. A dull first half in the next game against auld enemy Scotland offered little hope, but two iconic moments would change the game. England were 1-0 ahead through Alan Shearer when David Seaman famously saved Gary McAllister's penalty kick. Moments later, Paul Gascoigne provided his most iconic England goal, flicking the ball over Colin Hendry's head and volleying into the corner of the net. The whole country was off and running – Euro 96 was out of the blocks.

Then came one of the great England performances. Two goals each from Alan Shearer and Teddy Sheringham destroyed a Netherlands team laced with stars. Edwin van der Sar, Jaap Stam, Clarence Seedorf, Edgar Davids, Dennis Bergkamp and Patrick Kluivert were the biggest names in the squad. While still very young (Stam only had one cap when the tournament began) the Ajax contingent had just reached back-to-back Champions League finals, including the legendary 1995 victory against Milan. No one expected England to blitz the Dutch as they did, winning 4-1.

Spain were hugely unfortunate against England in the quarter-finals. In a drab game the Spaniards had two goals disallowed, at least one of which was certainly onside and incorrectly chalked off. England created very little throughout the 120 minutes, but come the penalty kicks, heroes would emerge. David Seaman, after his strong penalty stop in normal time against Scotland, would save two Spanish penalties. The key kick for England was number three, taken by Stuart Pearce. Pearce had missed dramatically against West Germany in the World Cup 1990 semi-final, striking his penalty with immense power down the middle of the goal. Bodo Illgner had dived past the ball but his trailing leg deflected it away. Against Spain Pearce arrowed his spot kick into the corner and provided an iconic celebration. Eyes popping, roaring at the top of his voice, his biceps bulged in a celebration of raw passion and redemption.

In the semi-final England would face a repeat of Italia 90. Germany was now stronger, reunified, and able to include former East German players such as Mathias Sammer. When Tony Adams flicked on Paul Gascoigne's corner, Alan Shearer pounced to head England into the lead. Germany equalised when Stefan Kuntz stretched and glided in a far-post effort. At half-time the score was 1-1, as it would be at full-time.

In extra time came two pivotal moments. First Darren Anderton hit the post with the goal at his mercy. Minutes later Alan Shearer volleyed the ball across the six-yard box – Gascoigne seemed to pause, unsure if the goalkeeper would intercept, then went again, sliding at full stretch. Surely with any firm touch it would have been a goal? Agonisingly, there was no contact and the ball trickled harmlessly wide. The penalty shoot-out followed, with England perfect until Gareth Southgate stroked his penalty low but not far enough to the left of Andreas Köpke. Germany went through to face the Czech Republic in the final, winning 2-1.

This 'what if' had three possible choices with seemingly similar outcomes. What if Anderton scores? What if Gascoigne makes good contact? What if Southgate converts his penalty?

If either Anderton or Gascoigne score Gareth Southgate is not put in the position of having to take a penalty – this potentially changes Southgate's personal story far more than if Southgate converts. If Southgate scores and Müller scores immediately after, the shoot-out merely continues, casting someone else in the hero or villain spot. Southgate's role is forgotten. He no longer has a redemptive story as England manager; indeed, he might never plough a managerial furrow with a different timeline of events.

Anderton's effort against the post occurred prior to Gascoigne's opportunity. Had he scored the game is 2-1 and the Gazza moment far less impactful. On a personal level the impact on Anderton personally would be far less significant than it would have been for Gascoigne.

Gascoigne's personal troubles after 1996 have been headline news. A cycle of addiction, rehabilitation and news headlines have followed him. His personality has been one of manic highs and extreme lows. Being the hero would have meant the world to Gazza. Already adored by the majority of the public, his status would have been assured had he been the player who scored the winner versus Germany to propel England into the final of Euro 96.

What of that match-up? England versus Czech Republic? The Czechs would push Germany all the way to extra time and a Bierhoff golden goal. They were not a team to be underestimated, but neither were they a dominant team. Drawn in the same group as Germany and Italy, they squeezed through. Germany topped the group with seven points from their three games. Italy and the Czech Republic finished level on points but the

Czechs made it through by virtue of a 2-1 win against Italy. Karel Poborský's iconic scooped lob was the only goal of the game against Portugal in the quarter-final. In the semi-final a dull 0-0 against a French team on the verge of greatness ended in penalties. The Czechs were perfect and Pedro missed the crucial sudden-death kick for France.

The Czech team were on the rise. Nedvěd, Poborský and Šmicer were all at Slavia Prague, ready to make their leap into the big time. Patrik Berger was officially still a Borussia Dortmund player but the deal to move to Liverpool had been done. Reaching this final was ahead of schedule for them.

England would have been well placed to beat them and win Euro 96, ending 30 years of hurt.

What happens next? There would surely be some form of domino effect from this victory. The status of all involved would be elevated to new levels. In England, where losing semi-finalists are held in great esteem, let alone those who actually win a trophy, Euro 96 made pop culture icons of many of the England team. Some sealed their legend because of their achievements in their playing careers after the tournament. Had England been victorious every player involved would have become iconic. Good servants of the game like Anderton and Southgate earn their own pedestal. Steve McManaman goes from a player who many undervalued to an unquestioned icon. Terry Venables left his position as England manager after the tournament, but with the glory of a tournament win these circumstances could change. Venables would become spoken of in the same terms as Sir Alf Ramsey, a managerial great in our midst. In all likelihood he takes the team to the World Cup in 1998.

The preparation for the 1998 tournament seemed to be going superbly under Glenn Hoddle. Until the squad announcement. Hoddle decided to leave out Paul Gascoigne. The impact this had on Gascoigne's life is, like everything else, open to speculation. What is for certain is that it was not long after the incident that Gascoigne checked into rehab.

If Venables is still in charge of the England team, does he exclude the player who scored the winner in the Euro 96 semi-final? Highly unlikely. An England team still buoyed by breaking the cycle of hurt, retaining the bonds of a tournament win and with the additional talents of Scholes, Beckham and Owen may better the last-16 loss against Argentina. Going how far? One can only imagine.

There are further potential issues with regards to this legacy – one tactical, the other cultural.

Venables' England used a flexible 3-5-2 formation that could become a back four if needed. Hoddle would also use a 3-5-2. The system would not be used by England again until Steve McClaren and then it would be shelved until Gareth Southgate found success using the shape. Winning has an influence on cultural perceptions. Once Ramsey won the World Cup without wingers that style swept through English football and took hold. Had England won with a 3-5-2 set-up then that would have become the official formation of English football. In the mid-1990s a number of clubs used a 3-5-2, notably Liverpool and Aston Villa. More would certainly have followed, all the way down to grassroots teams.

Notably it was the arrival of a foreign coach that saw England become once more wedded to 4-4-2. Sven-Göran Eriksson was appointed in 2001 following Kevin Keegan's resignation. The culture question to ask is: had England won a major tournament with an English manager, would they ever have decided to appoint a foreign coach? Might English success have further perpetuated a football culture that preferred to look inwards, rather than outwards or had the juggernaut of the Premier League already set the wheels of importing football talent in motion? In 1996 the Premier League was only four years old. The die had not been fully cast. The Premier League of the 2020s might be culturally less open, with more emphasis on domestic managers and players had Paul Gascoigne made contact and scored.

WHAT IF WE RESTRUCTURED ENGLISH FOOTBALL?

It is one of the great football quiz questions. Which is the only English club to have played in the Premier League, Division One, Two, Three, Four, Division Three North and Division Three South? (The answer is at the end of this chapter.)

The question illustrates how the English game has grown organically since the original 12 clubs from the North and Midlands formed the first Football League in 1888. In 2023 we have the Premier League, the Championship, League One and League Two. The Premier League has grown into one of the most valuable sports brands in the world. Since their introduction in 1987, the play-offs have provided excitement and emotion on an epic scale. But the current structure of English football also has its flaws and its perennial problems. So, what if we took a blank piece of paper and set out to restructure the English game once and for all? Although we do not have to take into account the history behind the FA or the Football League, nor their conflicting self-interests, we want to provide a viable solution, a template that works better.

There are a number of easily identifiable issues to address. Fixture congestion has been a challenge for clubs chasing honours as each season reaches its climax. It is also cited by managers as the reason their players sustain more muscle injuries through fatigue. For the top clubs, with the cushion of multi-million-pound television deals, reducing the number of games played should not have so much of an impact. It was stated shortly after one of the Premier League deals that each club could let every fan in for free and still have more money than they did previously. But at the lower levels of English football, the fans that arrive through the turnstiles are the financial lifeblood. Their club isn't a 'global brand'. Their club has a real place in the local community. There is no universal cure across the current structure for too many games. But the size of each league will be a major consideration as we set out our blueprint.

Wealthy clubs hire private jets, they stay in five-star hotels, they have the best of everything to ensure that their players arrive in top shape when they travel away to play fixtures. Again there is a sharp contrast here with clubs at the bottom end of the game. Away fixtures can eat up finances. Long coach journeys can affect performance. The effect on the environment, together with ever spiralling fuel costs add to the difficulties faced by current League One and Two clubs. It is also a huge consideration for the everyday football fan. The cost of following your team home and away has spiralled in recent years, even without overseas travel for those involved in European competition. Fans also love local derbies. The proximity of clubs builds rivalries, and not only between clubs from the same city or town. This will certainly be a consideration as we set out to reshape English football.

Cup games can provide different levels of excitement to regular league fixtures. The FA Cup was once the most famous cup competition in the world. It still holds a special place in the hearts of many older fans in England. For younger fans, it has fallen down the pecking order of trophies they want to see their club win, certainly for those fans of current Premier League clubs. The Football League Cup has always struggled for recognition, but became increasingly popular once it was given a showpiece final at Wembley. Yet it is still very much the least considered trophy even though it has been monopolised in recent years by clubs who regularly play in the Champions League. The English Football League Trophy for third- and fourth- tier clubs is often played to sparse attendances in its early rounds. Restoring the prestige to the English cup competitions is something we will certainly be evaluating.

We begin with the Premier League. What if we reduce the number of teams in the top tier in England? Both Serie A and La Liga have returned to a top division of 20 clubs, but we favour the Bundesliga version that has just 18. This immediately cuts four fixtures from a crowded list. Premier League teams can play up to seven games in December. We would retain the traditional Boxing Day fixtures but take out the midweek games, and also the midweek games played in Easter to help clubs chasing Champions League and FA Cup success. Given the amount of money generated through current television deals, and the likelihood that this is still on the increase, the loss of income from four matchdays should not inconvenience the Premier League clubs too much. With fewer players getting injured there is also a very good argument that the product would be enhanced too, through quality rather than quantity.

Many clubs have struggled financially once they have been relegated from the Premier League. This is the reason behind the 'parachute payments' that give those teams such an advantage in the current Championship. Many clubs have also 'bet the farm' in trying to get out of the second tier to the golden uplands of the Premier League. In recent times large clubs such as Leeds United, Sunderland and Derby County have all fallen into terrible financial difficulties. So, what if we create a second division, Premier League Two, again with 18 teams in it? There would now be 36 clubs under the Premier League 'brand'. The TV and media would have more games to broadcast. The additional money generated by the Premier League 'brand' would be distributed more evenly across the 36 clubs so that the 'parachute payments' would no longer be needed. We also feel Premier League Two would reduce the risk of clubs spending too wildly in the hope of reaching the Premier League. Poor financial management happens at every level of football. We could never eradicate it. But we hope this structure would help.

We have taken 16 clubs from the current Football League to make up Premier League Two. But what if we restore the Football League to its 92-club membership? We can do this by adding the 23 clubs from the current National Conference league together with the top 15 clubs from the current Conference North and Conference South divisions. And what if the divisions of the Football League were organised on a regional basis? Division One North and South each with 22 teams, and Division Two North and South each with 24 teams. As clubs at this level rely heavily on matchday income, we are happy to see more teams in these leagues than in the top two tiers. It would also mean Carlisle would not have to travel to Exeter, nor Barrow to Torquay. There would be more local derbies and less trailing around the country for clubs and fans. This should lower costs and increase both interest and income.

Before we outline our proposals for promotion and relegation we want to address the cup competitions in England. We believe the FA Cup should be returned to its former glory as the greatest knockout competition in the world. Elevating the levels of prize money is one way to do this, but this would rely on the FA recruiting very generous sponsors. So what if the winners of the FA Cup were awarded a place in the Champions League? This would without doubt not only restore prestige, but also add value to the competition. A team having a poor run in the league would still have a real incentive through the FA Cup. The draw would continue in its present form on a national basis from the first qualifying round. This would allow for teams in the lower leagues, now organised in our structure on a North and South basis, to compete against each other in one-off ties, without it becoming cost prohibitive. The concept of David versus Goliath is a key element in the attraction of the FA Cup.

We would abolish the English Football League Trophy. It seems to generate little interest even in the lower leagues until the regional semi-final stages. But the idea of a lower-league club having a day out at Wembley is a good one. So, what if we keep the Football League Cup, for Football League teams only? The current Premier League clubs rarely take the competition seriously until the semi-final stage and yet still manage to monopolise it. A cup competition for teams in our new Football League only would give lower-league clubs a tangible chance of success.

In our newly created Premier League One and Two we have 32 clubs. Of these, seven will be involved in European football. To aid these seven clubs in their European quests we have reduced the number of league fixtures they play. For the 25 other teams we can see there could be a shortage of fixtures, especially if a team makes an early exit from the FA Cup. So, what if we introduce a Premier League Cup for the 25 teams not in Europe? To give this some value and prestige we would award the winners a place in the Europa Conference League.

So to the spoils and the end-of-season excitement. The play-offs have been an undoubted success since their introduction. They would be retained with some slight tweaks to the format. Our view is that the top team in each division should always be promoted. But what if we allow a team at the bottom end of the table to try save its season through the play-offs, as they do in the Bundesliga? In a Premier League of just 18 teams, it would reduce anxieties about a smaller division and offer clubs an opportunity to show they deserve their place.

So how does promotion and relegation work in our new template for English football? The Premier League winners, runners-up and third-placed team would go into the Champions League. As outlined previously the fourth place would go to the FA Cup winners. Teams finishing fourth and fifth in our new top tier would qualify for the Europa League. The winners of our new Premier League Cup would qualify for the Europa Conference League. Should the FA Cup be won by a top-three team, then places would be adjusted accordingly based on league positions. The bottom two clubs would be relegated.

The top team from Premier League Two would be promoted automatically. The next six teams would play off 2v7, 3v6 and 4v5 in quarter-finals. The winners would join the team finishing 16th in Premier League One in semi-finals, with the final at Wembley deciding who takes the last place in the top tier the following season. This should create enormous interest throughout the season given that the team finishing seventh has a chance of promotion. A half-decent run could take a team lying 13th or 14th at Christmas to the play-off places. The bottom two clubs in Premier League Two would be relegated.

Both the winners of Division One North and the winners of Division One South would be promoted to Premier League Two. The teams placed second to seventh in each division would play off. The three winners from Division One North would then play the three winners of Division One South in quarter-finals. These three winners would be joined by the team finishing 16th in Premier League Two in the play-off semi-finals. The winners would face each other in the final at Wembley to determine who takes the last place in Premier League Two. The bottom three clubs from both Division One North and Division One South would be relegated.

The top three clubs from both Division Two North and Division Two South would be promoted. The teams placed fourth, fifth and sixth in Division Two North would be joined by the team finishing 21st in Division One North in play-off semi-finals, with the winners playing in each final at Wembley for the final place in Division One North. The same format would apply to Division One South. The bottom two teams in each of

Divisions Two North and South would be relegated out of the Football League.

So we posed the question 'What if we start with a blank sheet of paper and restructure English football?' Our aims? To reduce fixture congestion towards the climax of the season. To grow and strengthen the Premier League while reducing the risks of relegation from it. To increase the financial viability of clubs in tiers three and four by making them regional, creating more local interest and reducing costly travel. To restore the FA Cup to its former glory.

We believe all of the changes we would make would enhance the experience of football for both players and fans alike.

QUIZ QUESTION ANSWER: Coventry City.

WHAT IF MICHAEL OWEN
HAD STAYED FIT?

At the end of 2001 Michael Owen stood with five trophies and the Ballon d'Or, voted as the best footballer in Europe. He was just 21 years old.

Owen had packed more into the first four years of his career than many footballers achieve in 15. After one season in the Liverpool first team Owen was included in the England squad for the 1998 World Cup. His first game at the tournament came against Romania, coming off the bench to score. In the knockout stages his reputation was made, scoring a sensational solo goal against Argentina. Owen followed up by winning his second Golden Boot as Premier League top scorer, but it was the 2000/01 season that propelled Owen to the very top. Liverpool would win an unprecedented treble of FA Cup, League Cup and UEFA Cup, with Owen's goals vital to the success. Especially memorable would be the 'Owen final' in the FA Cup. With Liverpool outplayed by Arsenal for much of the game and trailing, Owen poached an equaliser before his trademark pace and acceleration surged him into a position to stroke a left-footed winning goal across

David Seaman. Liverpool would add the Community Shield and European Super Cup at the beginning of the 2001/02 season, completing their five-trophy collection.

Unfortunately for Owen, as well as packing in success, he also suffered injuries. Injuries that would seriously impact the trajectory of his career. Owen's first big setback was a hamstring problem against Leeds in April 1999. He would be out for five months. A series of smaller issues plagued Owen throughout 1999. Then in January of 2000 his hamstring went again. He stayed relatively trouble-free until an ankle injury against Arsenal in 2003 sidelined him for three months. After his retirement Owen admitted that the prospect of getting injured was always on his mind and impacted his performance.

He would leave Liverpool in 2004 to join Real Madrid, where he stayed relatively healthy but saw his playing time limited by the presence of Raúl and Ronaldo (R9). In 2005 Owen signed for Newcastle. He damaged his thigh not long after arriving, found fitness but then broke a metatarsal. He returned for the 2006 World Cup, where he would suffer the biggest injury of his career rupturing his anterior cruciate ligament (ACL). Owen would not recover for almost a full year. By the time he returned the electric, devastating Owen of the turn of the century had gone. He had scored at a fine rate of 26 goals in 71 games. He missed the whole of the 2006/07 season due to the ACL. Newcastle were relegated. Had he stayed fit they likely would have avoided this fate.

Michael Owen remained a tremendous penalty box predator even after his injuries, but he was no longer capable of leaving the Argentine defence in his wake as he did in 1998. He was capable of scoring and creating goals out of nothing thanks to his incredible ability to go from standing to sprinting in the blink of an eye. With those hamstring issues such motion invited further complications.

Could they have been avoided?

In 2021 a good comparison would be another Liverpool goalscoring hero, Mohamed Salah. Salah's turn of speed has been crucial to his success without him experiencing anything close to Owen's level of injury problems. Following a stunning goal against Chelsea he struck a yoga pose as his celebration. When asked about this, Salah declared himself 'a yoga guy', crediting his flexibility to his regular yoga sessions. Almost 30 years earlier Ryan Giggs was running down the wing for Manchester United but experiencing hamstring woes. Giggs would also turn to yoga, decreasing the number of hamstring troubles for the rest of his career. Giggs retired months before his 39th birthday. His electric pace had deserted him by then, but this was due to age rather than injury.

What might have happened if Michael Owen had been persuaded to take up yoga after his first hamstring injury?

In 1999 Owen was injured in April against Leeds. He had 18 goals at that stage and still won a Golden Boot despite missing Liverpool's last seven league games.

Liverpool lost three of those and would finish the season in seventh place. A fit Owen might have meant Liverpool won more of the remaining games but with Champions League qualification for only the top three teams it is unlikely to have made a significant difference. It was the archetypal transitional season. Liverpool experimented with joint managers in Roy Evans and Gérard Houllier, but Evans would leave in November, leaving Houllier in sole charge. At the end of the season Steve McManaman left for Real Madrid. However, a young player by the name of Steven Gerrard had appeared 13 times for the first team. The 1996 FA Youth Cup-winning trio of Owen, Gerrard and Jamie Carragher were about to cement their presence in the Liverpool first team.

The following season Liverpool managed to finish fourth in the Premier League, missing out on the Champions League by just two points. Liverpool failed to win any of their last five league games, qualifying for the UEFA Cup. Had Owen avoided injury in January, Liverpool might have finished higher in the table. However, had they done so they would not have been in the UEFA Cup, the treble of League Cup, FA Cup and UEFA Cup in 2001 could not have happened, and the events that created Owen's Ballon d'Or would not have taken place. Manchester United finished the season as champions with 91 points, 24 ahead of Liverpool. It is highly unlikely a fully fit Owen would have had an impact on the title picture.

For the next three seasons Owen remained fit and Liverpool were on the rise. Liverpool had bought well, adding international players to the home-grown ranks. They had a strong array of forwards in Owen, Fowler and Heskey. Steven Gerrard's status increased as he played a key role in the treble season. During that 2001 campaign Liverpool qualified for the Champions League, which they followed up with a second-place finish in 2002. During this time it would be Steven Gerrard who suffered with injuries, leading to him missing the 2002 World Cup.

While Owen and Liverpool's league performances may not have improved very much during this period had he remained fully fit, his goal tally surely would have. It is a strange statistical quirk that not once in his career did Michael Owen reach 20 league goals in a single season. At Liverpool he scored 19 twice, 18 twice and 16 twice. In many of these seasons he didn't complete 30 league games – had he done so, 20 would have been beaten with ease.

In 2003/04 Liverpool finished fourth, qualifying for the Champions League. Owen scored 16 league goals in 29 games. Liverpool were 15 points off third place, so once more it is doubtful his fitness would have made up the gap. By this stage the injuries and a lack of league title challenge had ground Owen down and he decided it was time to move on. The appointment of Rafa Benítez was not enough to convince him that things were about to change. In 2004/05 he joined Real Madrid, missing out on Liverpool's Champions League triumph.

It is conceivable that without the major physical obstacles Owen's time at Liverpool would have been different. The treble season might never have happened, but he would certainly have broken the 20-goal barrier on at least two occasions and possibly have claimed another Golden Boot. Owen might have chosen to remain at the club rather than looking for change. Liverpool would then have had the benefit of an apex Steven Gerrard plus a fully fit and firing Michael Owen.

During the years when Liverpool sought to mount title challenges they seemed to be reliant on individual players at various times; when they had players operating in tandem the title challenges emerged. In 2001 Liverpool had a squad full of players who were able to contribute at vital moments. In 2002 that continued, but after that they seemed to rely on Michael Owen. It was a heavy burden for a player fighting injuries. When Owen left they relied on Steven Gerrard until the arrival of Fernando Torres. The Gerrard and Torres partnership is what Gerrard and Owen might have been had Michael Owen stayed fit and stayed at Liverpool. Liverpool only received £8.5 million for Owen and Torres arrived three years later, so it is not impossible to imagine that Liverpool could have retained Owen and still signed Torres. An Owen, Gerrard and Torres axis would certainly have given Premier League defenders something to think about.

When Michael Owen left Liverpool he was 25 years old and had scored 158 club goals in 297 games. His final career haul was 222 goals in 482 games. Owen retired aged 34. In the nine years after leaving Liverpool he only managed a total of 64 goals. Had he stayed fit and remained at Anfield it is a not unreasonable assumption that Owen would have ended with a figure much closer to 350 goals, with 400 not impossible.

Owen's injury also fundamentally impacted his England career. He scored 40 times for England; only five men have scored more. He was 28 years old when he played his final England game. A fully fit Michael Owen has four or five more years of international football and more than enough opportunities to surpass 50 England goals, possibly even setting a number that Wayne Rooney was unable to break. Owen's fitness also has a direct impact on the 2006 World Cup. His injury occurred in the first game of the tournament. Without one of their key players England reached the quarter-finals, losing on penalties following a 0-0 draw with Portugal. Would the extra firepower of an apex Michael Owen have helped England into the semi-final?

WHAT IF SOCCER HAD BECOME THE NATIONAL SPORT OF THE USA?

The favourite sport of the United States is American football. The National Football League is the most watched and most valuable in the world. The Super Bowl has become almost an unofficial national holiday, an occasion of pomp and ceremony, of glamour and glitz, the like of which only America can do. Basketball has the most participants with almost one in ten Americans playing the game, and a court within easy distance of everyone. Baseball is seen as the 'nation's pastime', especially during the summer months. 'Soccer' lags behind in fourth in terms of 'favourite sport'. The greatest nation in the world and the greatest game in the world have never seemed to fully embrace.

This hierarchy has a significant impact on who plays which sport and how much success is achieved from it. The kudos, the celebrity, the monetary rewards that come with playing at elite level, usually dictate where youngsters, generally good at a number of sports, concentrate their aspirations and their efforts. Success over a period of time becomes self-perpetuating. In New Zealand, to be an All Black is still the ultimate ambition. In India and Pakistan it is cricket that is undoubtedly the nation's number one sport. In the vast majority of other nations around the globe it is football that attracts those with athleticism, coordination, balance and vision. Yet in the USA, the most kudos, the most recognition, comes from playing American football.

There have been any number of theories as to why soccer has never totally grabbed the imagination of the American public. Most seem to post-rationalise without looking too deep. *It isn't part of the culture. There is not enough scoring and too many games end in a draw. More people would watch and play if the national team was more successful.* All part of the rich debate. Especially when taking into account the rise in popularity of women's soccer in the last 30 years, where the national team's success has certainly played a huge part in the game's growing popularity. Yet if we do start to look deeper, if we do explore the history of 'football' in the USA, the development of the different versions of the game follow a very similar path to those in England. Not only that, but there appears to be an almost pivotal moment when 'soccer' in the United States could have become more popular than 'football'.

Immigrants brought association football over from England in the 1860s and of course they also brought with them rugby football. Like in England there was a blurring of the two codes in those early days as the laws of both games evolved. Eventually, as in England, there was a separation, as association football became 'soccer' and 'football' became the American version of rugby.

By the 1880s the game played with a round ball became more organised and the early incarnation of governance came in the form of the American Football Association (AFA). It sought to standardise a set of rules and create competitions for its member clubs, including the first cup competition, the American Cup. Given the sheer size and scale of the USA it is no surprise to learn that other leagues sprang up in different parts of the country. And it comes as no surprise to learn that these leagues had differences of opinion about how the game should be governed. It was the American Amateur Football Association (AAFA) that emerged to challenge the AFA. Both applied to FIFA to be the national governing body in 1913. Eventually it was the AAFA that gained the upper hand and changed its name to the United States Football Association (USFA). By this time soccer was seen as second only to baseball as the nation's favourite sport.

There was still more acrimony to come, however, and like in England it became a stand-off between the governing body and the leagues that ran the game week by week. Just as the big clubs in the north of England challenged the southern-based FA and formed the Football League in 1888, so the American Soccer League (ASL) challenged the USFA in the 1920s. With many of its clubs based in the north-east, the ASL was arguably the strongest league in the US. Its clubs were able to attract professional players, some full internationals from England and Scotland to play, something that was frowned upon at the time by FIFA.

As ever, finances became the focal point of the dispute. In England it had been the distinction between the amateur and the professional player that had been the cause of the disagreement. Eventually the FA backed down and allowed professionals to play in its famous cup competition. In the USA it was the ASL which objected to its teams being required to play in the USFA's National Challenge Cup, as the travel involved caused financial hardship. On two separate occasions the ASL boycotted the National Challenge Cup. The USFA did what any organisation would do in the midst of what became known as America's 'Soccer Wars': in 1930 it set up a league to rival the ASL, the Eastern Professional Soccer League. It had the desired effect. Clubs began to desert the ASL and by 1933 it had gone.

With the 20/20 vision that hindsight brings, this period of 1900 to 1930 is when soccer missed its opportunity in the USA. In England there had been similar disputes and clashes of egos between the people who governed the game. Luckily there were men with vision who saw how to bring different factions together as one. They were helped, no doubt, by the fact that England is only the size of one of the larger states in America, and that organising the game in the days before air travel was so much easier. The FA Cup became the most famous cup competition in the world and the Football League expanded rapidly from 12 clubs in 1888 to 92 clubs by 1921.

Yet if US soccer had challenges to face, they were nothing compared to American football. In 1905 the headline of the *Chicago Sunday* Tribune announced **'Football Year's Death Harvest – Record Shows That Nineteen Players Have Been Killed; One Hundred Thirty-seven Hurt – Two Are Slain Saturday'**. Deaths on the field were a regular occurrence as football made its transition from rugby. Even so, the game continued to thrive, not least in the universities and colleges.

Violence has its attraction but such was the carnage on the fields where football was played that President Roosevelt stepped in. Roosevelt was a fan of football: **'I believe in rough games and in rough, manly sports. I do not feel any particular sympathy for the person who gets battered about a good deal so long as it is not fatal.'** The problem was, however, that American football *was* fatal. Some colleges stopped playing altogether. Even Harvard, one of the game's great advocates, was close to dropping the game. The Harvard president Charles Eliot was quoted as saying that football was **'more brutalising than prizefighting, cockfighting or bullfighting'**.

Using his legendary powers of diplomacy, Roosevelt managed to get the game's administrators around the table to look at how football might change to make it less dangerous. The rules were amended. The famous 'flying wedge' where players linked arms and charged was outlawed. Progress on the field was altered from four downs in five yards to three. The biggest change was the introduction of the forward pass, which separated the game once and for all from its rugby forerunner. Protective helmets, usually made from leather and not dissimilar to a rugby skull cap, were now a regular feature of the game, although nowhere near as effective as their modern-day versions. The result was that in the following two years, 1906 and 1907, there were *only* 11 fatalities per season.

The pivotal moment appeared to have come in 1930. Despite the intervention of a president and changes to its rules, the *New York Times* announced **'40 Players Killed In Football Season'.** Contrast this to the performance of the USA 'soccer team' in the inaugural World Cup that year. The United States beat Belgium and Paraguay to top their group, eventually losing in the semi-final to Argentina. A more than creditable performance. Surely this had to be the moment that 'soccer' became more popular than 'football'? It wasn't to be. Soccer lost its way just as it was becoming a huge spectator sport. The Americans resented constant interventions from the ruling body FIFA, and didn't like their game being governed from abroad. Many of its clubs were funded by industry and the Great Depression took its toll with companies no longer able to offer their support.

American football, on the other hand, continued to evolve through rule changes and grow in popularity. Its administrators set about organising a clearly understandable format with the two divisions, East and West. The winners of these divisions played in a final to decide the national champions. It began to get more and more coverage in the national newspapers. American football had far to travel to the recognised format of today, with its well-established franchises in the American Football Conference and the National Football Conference playing off for the ultimate glory in the Super Bowl, but it was off and running towards capturing the sporting hearts of the nation.

But what if soccer had built on its World Cup success? What if 'Soccer Wars' had ceased, and the game had become administered by men of vision? What if young players had grown up wanting to be Bert Patenaude, Bart McGee and Billy Gonsalves, the stars of the 1930 USA World Cup squad, instead of Earl Clark, Cliff Battles and Ken Strong, the stars of 1930s American football? Every youngster has their heroes, and sport often provides them. If soccer becomes the game in the States with the highest status and most kudos, everything changes. Those who show talent in one sport are inevitably good at a variety of games or disciplines. In England it is rare for a youngster with an option to compete at a number of elite level sports to choose any other over football. There are many skills that are transferable from one sport to another, not least the ability of superstar players to find moments of space and time in the chaos of a team sport. It's not difficult to see America producing soccer wingers with the dribbling skills of Magic Johnson or Stephen Curry. Or central midfielders with the vision of quarterbacks like Tom Brady or Dan Marino. Or strikers with the speed and elusive running of wide receivers like Jerry Rice and Randy Moss. If American soccer had started to attract its brightest and best young sportsmen from the 1930s onwards, its impact would have been seismic.

If 'Soccer Wars' had ended and 'Soccer Peace' had broken out, how would the game have organised itself? Would it have had a recognised 'pyramid' system as in England? The larger states in the USA are very similar in population to many European countries. In England football administration has always been split between the FA County Football Associations and the Football League, so it's reasonable to suggest that each state might have eventually developed a league pyramid that fed into a national league. Yet soccer has always flourished in the major cities around the world. As travel became easier and the post-war boom arrived, it is most likely that the big cities would have grouped together and formed a league similar to the one that exists now as Major League Soccer. America always seems to organise its sports on an East and West basis and does so today with soccer. Given the size of the country and the distances travelled the

Major Soccer League almost mirrors the much derided European Super League that has been mooted in recent years. For Manchester, Madrid and Milan read Chicago, Columbus and Colorado.

The US always grasped the notion of professionalism with more vindication and confidence than Europe and most certainly Britain. Even in the 1920s and 30s America was attracting footballers from England and Scotland to play by offering greater wage incentives. The maximum wage in football in England was only abolished in 1961. Pressure from the States, with talent crossing the Atlantic, would surely have seen this happen earlier. The 1960s saw star players like Denis Law and Jimmy Greaves move to Italy. It is much more likely stars like these would have moved to America given that there would have been no language barrier.

If America is producing its own star players, if the American league is now one of the strongest in the world, then for certain their players would have been paid more than in Europe. America saw the potential of business and sport long before its European counterparts. The introduction of the European Cup in 1955 brought an added glamour to competition on the continent and the major clubs now had another sizeable income stream. Yet in the sphere of sports coverage, of television rights and player deals, money always talks and America always seems to be two steps ahead of Europe. The deal for 2023 with YouTube worth £11.5 billion is further proof. So it is most likely the talent drain from Britain would have accelerated, if anything.

American football was televising live games on Saturday nights as early as 1953. It took another 30 years for this to happen in England. The American leagues would have been able to attract the star players from other countries too. Brazilians and Argentinians have graced soccer in England, Spain and Italy, but given what America would have offered it is most likely they would have plied their trade in the US.

Only one thing would have stopped the talent drain of players to America. The FA, the Football League and the owners of the big clubs would have bowed to commercial pressure. They would have had to realise the potential of their 'product' and its revenue streams or see their game steadily decline. The rights to televise football were virtually given away up to this point. There was still an almost amateur approach to off-field business. There would have been some interesting conversations with the BBC and ITV. For too long the only live football seen on television was the FA Cup Final and the home internationals. The BBC's *Match of the Day* would screen highlights from a couple of matches and it was the same with ITV's *Soccer Sunday*. To keep the star players in Britain from crossing over to America, clubs would have had to have recognised the need to promote and exploit the great desire among fans to watch live football on television. The most likely outcome is that we would have seen the Premier League arrive not in 1992 but around 20 years earlier.

Success at international level for a country the size of the USA with soccer as its national sport would have been inevitable; it is only the pervading culture that is preventing it now. The World Club Championship that was once a play-off between the champions of South America and the champions of Europe has developed into a four-club tournament with the addition of teams from other continents. There is now talk of a World Club Cup with up to 32 teams competing. It is much more likely that this would have developed into a three-way competition between South America, Europe and the USA as the United States Soccer Federation grew in stature and the US teams became stronger and more dominant.

The strength of the USA national team would most certainly have been felt at the World Cup too. At present the axis of success is split between Europe with 12 World Cup wins and South America with ten. Europe's total population is around a third more than that of the USA, but Croatia, with their population of fewer than four million people, have reached a World Cup Final. If American soccer had come to the fore as a sport by the 1960s it is not unreasonable to suggest that the USA would have won at least three World Cups by now.

So far we have not ventured into women's soccer in the USA. All we have to do to add any credibility to the theories ventured above is to look in this direction. Soccer is the team sport most played by women in the US and there are 1.7 million registered players. The women's national team has a higher profile in the States than the men's due to its success on the field. So far there have been eight Women's World Cups and the USA has won four of them.

If soccer had become the favourite sport for men in the USA in the 1930s it would have changed the hierarchy in the game on a national and international level beyond all recognition.

WHAT IF ROMAN ABRAMOVICH BUYS SPURS INSTEAD OF CHELSEA?

The bounce of a ball. Fortunes can be lost and made on the bounce of a ball. Rattling from red to black and the dreaded double zero. Many a fortune has been swallowed up by the double zero at Les Ambassadeurs.

Wealth drips from the very walls of Les Ambassadeurs casino in central London, a mere ten-minute walk from Buckingham Palace. Money comes and goes as if it is of little significance. Losing tens of thousands is no drama here. The rich intermingle and opportunities to do business pervade.

A suave Swedish gentleman sashays through the casino. He doesn't try to draw attention to himself but everyone knows who he is. The fingers of his hand sweep back well-groomed grey hair before adjusting high-end designer glasses. Furtive glances around the casino betray the fact that he is looking intently for someone.

Tucked away in a corner are two sharply dressed gentlemen and a more casually dressed man. They don't have the air of Englishmen. Or of Swedes. These men have a look of Eastern Europe. Tough, rugged and weathered, but this is 2003. They also look moneyed. Dapper suits, designer clothing and gold accessories. The Swede knows he has found who he is looking for.

He introduces himself to the sharpest-dressed of the men. It is the casually dressed man who responds. Sven-Göran Eriksson, the manager of England in 2003, has just introduced himself to Roman Abramovich's driver, instead of the super-rich Russian he has been invited to meet.

Global events have meant that the reputations of certain individuals evolve over time, sometimes for the better and sometimes for the worse. This doesn't change the historical impact that the actions of a specific individual had on past events, though the prism through which these events are viewed may change.

Without any doubt Roman Abramovich's purchase of Chelsea was a seismic moment.

When Sven met with Roman the purchase of an English club was not the topic of conversation. Abramovich wanted to buy a Moscow club. Roman took Sven with him as he toured the clubs. Days later Abramovich had decided he no longer wanted to buy a Moscow club. His attention had switched to London. The question was 'Tottenham or Chelsea?' Sven advised that Chelsea were better positioned to win trophies.

Abramovich spent £140 million to buy Chelsea in 2003. The amount was split between £60 million for the club and £80 million to clear the club's debts. Chelsea had a cash injection in the early 1990s when Matthew Harding joined the club as a director. His investments purchased the freehold of Stamford Bridge and built a new stand, named after Harding, as well as considerable transfer funds. Chelsea's status began to rise as star names arrived; Ruud Gullit and Gianluca Vialli signed as players who would both go on to manage the club. Harding would die in a helicopter crash in 1996, but his family would continue to invest in the club.

Chelsea were consistent in the league, finishing no lower than sixth between 1996/97 and 2002/03, when Abramovich purchased the club. In 2000 Claudio Ranieri was attracted to Chelsea as a replacement for the outgoing Gianluca Vialli. Ranieri had taken Valencia into the Champions League and helped assemble an exciting, attacking team. Ranieri would help Chelsea finish fourth in 2002/03, with a crucial final day win against Liverpool edging them into the Champions League. It would be in July of 2003 that Abramovich took over the club.

Chelsea would immediately splash the cash. Damien Duff signed from Blackburn for £17 million; Hernan Crespo from Inter for virtually the same fee. Claude Makélélé joined from Real Madrid for £16 million; Adrian Mutu from Parma for £16 million; Juan Sebastain Veron from Manchester United for £15 million; Scott Parker from Charlton for £10 million and Joe Cole from West Ham for £6 million. In all Chelsea signed 14 players during the season for over £110 million. This at a time when the British transfer record was £30 million, spent by Manchester United on Rio Ferdinand.

Ranieri's Chelsea would finish second, a huge 21 points behind Arsenal's Invincibles. In the Champions League they were knocked out by Didier Deschamps' Monaco at the semi-final stage. Monaco would lose the final 3-0 against Porto, managed by José Mourinho.

For Abramovich second place would not do. He acted swiftly, going after the man who had captured the Champions League. More money was spent in the summer of 2004, assembling a team that Mourinho would manage to Premier League glory. That summer Chelsea bought fewer players but the players they did sign would be significant. Didier Drogba for £24 million; Ricardo Carvalho for £20 million; Paulo Ferreira for £13 million; Arjen Robben for £12 million and Petr Čech for £7 million all arrived that summer. Mourinho would win back-to-back Premier League titles.

Abramovich's time at Chelsea lasted nearly 19 years. During that period Chelsea won 21 trophies, including two Champions League titles. Over £2 billion was spent in the transfer market. Investments were also made off the pitch. In 2007 Chelsea opened the state-of-the-art training ground at Cobham. Many times plans for a new stadium emerged but Chelsea remain at Stamford Bridge.

The ownership of Tottenham Hotspur is a little more complicated as the club belonged to its shareholders. Alan

Sugar was the majority shareholder for over 15 years. ENIC International purchased 27 per cent of the club in 1991 and slowly increased their percentage over the following years to become the clear majority shareholders. At the time of Abramovich's interest in buying Spurs Sugar still had a significant stake in the club. It is possible that an Abramovich purchase would have been long and protracted, but a purchase was still possible.

How were Spurs performing circa 2003? Average. Spurs, in Premier League terms, were very average.

In 2002/03 Spurs were managed by Glenn Hoddle and had finished tenth in the Premier League. The previous season they had finished ninth under Hoddle. Glenn Hoddle became Spurs manager in April of the previous season, finishing 12th. The club had won its last trophy in 1999, winning the League Cup.

The 2002/03 squad was packed with veterans. Darren Anderton. Teddy Sheringham. Gustavo Poyet. Their bright hope was a young defender, Ledley King, and a player signed in the summer from Leeds United, Robbie Keane. The squad would be in need of a massive overhaul.

Roman Abramovich would certainly have the money to bring in whoever the manager wanted, but who would the manager be? Hoddle would no longer be the manager of Tottenham by September 2003 even in the real timeline. It is almost certain that Abramovich would move for a new manager. A big name to help attract the stars.

In 2003 there were plenty of possible contenders.

At the end of the 2002/03 season Real Madrid decided to part company with Vicente del Bosque. Del Bosque had won the La Liga title with Real, but just days after clinching the championship Madrid 'went in a different direction'. For a new owner looking to make a mark in European football the manager of the Galacticos would surely be most tempting.

In the summer of 2003 Marcello Lippi was halfway through his second period as Juventus manager. Lippi had been successful with the Grand Old Lady during the 1990s, winning three Serie A titles and reaching three straight Champions League finals, winning one in 1995/96. He went from Juventus to Inter, but then returned in 2001. The summer of 2002/03 had seen Lippi win a further Serie A and reach the 2002/03 Champions League Final. He would leave Juventus in 2004 for the job of Italy manager, winning the 2006 World Cup. A manager with great pedigree, sure to be on Abramovich's list.

Both sides of *El Clásico* changed manager in 2003. Barcelona had an extraordinarily poor run and found themselves as low as 12th place in January. Manager and board decided to go their separate ways, thus ended Louis van Gaal's second period in charge of Barcelona. Van Gaal had won three Eredivisie titles with Ajax and most significantly won the 1994/95 Champions League. In 1997 Van Gaal arrived at Barcelona, winning two La Liga titles before taking the Netherlands job for one year in 2001. The possession-based, winning style of Ajax and

Barcelona were still fresh in the minds of supporters and players. Roman Abramovich wanted to both win and entertain. Entertaining football has always been in the expectations of Spurs fans; Van Gaal could have been in the picture.

As soon as Abramovich had the chance at Chelsea he replaced Claudio Ranieri. He replaced him with the manager who was the reigning Champions League winner. In 2002/03 AC Milan had beaten Juventus on penalties, winning Carlo Ancelotti the first of his Champions League titles as manager. The Milan team contained players who would achieve legendary status: Paolo Maldini, Alessandro Nesta, Andrea Pirlo, Clarence Seedorf, Rui Costa and, significantly, Andriy Shevchenko. Abramovich was a huge Shevchenko fan, paying a record fee to eventually bring him to Chelsea. Shevchenko would depart Chelsea just as Ancelotti arrived, narrowly missing out on reuniting the pair. Abramovich could have the opportunity to appoint Ancelotti and bring in Shevchenko while still at the top of his game.

Abramovich appoints Ancelotti as the new manager of Tottenham Hotspur.

With Ancelotti as manager who would Spurs sign? They would have no European football to attract top players, just a top quality manager and huge amounts of cash. Spurs' 2002/03 squad was in desperate need of an overhaul. Kasey Keller was the first-choice goalkeeper, while Stephen Carr, Mauricio Taricco, Goran Bunjevčević and Ledley King racked up the most appearances in defence. Simon Davies on the wing played the most games in midfield, followed by Gus Poyet, otherwise selection lacked real consistency. In attack Teddy Sheringham, who would be 37 years old by the end of the season, appeared the most times. Robbie Keane played fewer games than Sheringham, but scored one goal more, with 13 to Sheringham's 12.

The squad is ripe for overhauling. Only Carr (who made the PFA team of the season in 2002/03), King and Keane are worthy of remaining as first-choice players. Given that Chelsea made 14 signings in Abramovich's first season at the club it is highly likely Spurs would do the same.

Some signings would be identical. Some transfers would be impacted by Ancelotti's preference for playing a narrow 4-4-2 diamond. This would mean that although Damien Duff was one of the hottest properties in English football at that time, Carlo Ancelotti would have little use for a winger. Claude Makélélé was a key transfer in for Chelsea from Real Madrid. He would be ideal to sit at the base of Ancelotti's diamond. Would he be lured to Spurs from Real Madrid with no Champions League football? Highly doubtful.

The moves for Scott Parker, Wayne Bridge, Joe Cole and Glen Johnson would all make perfect sense for Spurs. These provide a new central midfield who can operate at the base of the diamond or in a box-to-box role (Parker) and a new left-back with overlapping qualities to provide width to Ancelotti's system (Bridge). Joe Cole offers an attacking option behind the front two. While Johnson was widely heralded as one of the best prospects of the era, he provides cover at right-back plus being a long-term prospect.

This only adds three players to the starting XI to go with Carr, King and Keane. The team is still in need of a goalkeeper, central defender, two midfielders and a striker.

Spurs move for a goalkeeper. Paul Robinson joined Spurs in 2004 from Leeds United. Robinson would be England's first-choice goalkeeper between 2003 and 2007. He cost Spurs £2.5 million in May 2004. Spurs move for him a year early, securing the future England number one.

In central defence Spurs could make a move for then Ajax player Cristian Chivu. Chivu was highly regarded and would eventually win the Champions League with Inter Milan, but only after a spell at Roma that began in 2003. Spurs would be well positioned to sign Chivu for a fee somewhere between £10 million and £20 million. Chivu is Ledley King's new central defensive partner.

West Ham were raided by many clubs in this era. Their youth system helped many young players into the first team and into the England set-up. In 2004 Spurs moved to sign Michael Carrick from West Ham. Now, with Abramovich's money available they sign him a season earlier, slotting his deep playmaking abilities into the base of Ancelotti's midfield diamond. Carrick's fee in 2004 was under £4 million. There would likely be some inflation due to the oligarch billions.

The Tottenham midfield remains in need of creativity and depth. Two more signings would be required to get this team to the Champions League qualification levels.

Real Sociedad are a historic club in Spain. They have won the top division, but since Barcelona and Real Madrid have sprinted away from the rest of the pack the best they have been able to do is achieve Champions League qualification. They qualified for the Champions League by finishing second in the 2002/03 season. In the centre of their midfield was Xabi Alonso. Liverpool moved for Alonso in the summer of 2004, paying a fee of over £10 million. Spurs move for him in our 2003 timeline, adding a future World Cup and European Championship winner to their squad. Alonso, Carrick and Parker provide a core of quality passers capable of playing deeper midfield roles, but the squad still lacks goal threat and creativity.

A strong option comes from the midfield of Lazio. Lazio had finished fourth in Serie A but had slipped from their championship contending status of a few seasons earlier. One of their outstanding midfielders was Dejan Stanković. A highly versatile and creative midfielder, Stanković could slot into the midfield in any of the advanced roles. He would even be capable of playing the more defensive midfield role.

The recruitment now requires a quality striker to play alongside Robbie Keane. For the second time Ajax have the best candidate. In the summer of 2004 Juventus signed Zlatan Ibrahimović from Ajax. Zlatan came close to joining Premier League teams on a number of occasions before eventually signing for Manchester United in 2016. By signing in 2003 he joins aged 21 and can be a key player for Tottenham for years to come. Though not yet scoring goals at a rate of better than one goal every two games, Zlatan's physicality and style of play would be perfect for the Premier League. Despite not having Champions League football the lure of London and high wages would likely be enough to attract a young Zlatan from Amsterdam to White Hart Lane.

With these new signings, Spurs under Ancelotti line up with Paul Robinson in goal, Wayne Bridge at left-back, Stephen Carr at right-back, and Ledley King and Cristian Chivu in central defence. At the base of the midfield diamond is Michael Carrick. Xabi Alonso and Scott Parker play centrally with Dejan Stankovic behind the forwards. Zlatan Ibrahimovic and Robbie Keane form a strike partnership.

The team is very strong but also very young – the age and experience would be on the bench in Gus Poyet, Darren Anderton, Jamie Redknapp, Dean Richards and Christian Ziege. Though these players all suffered with injury they would still offer some depth to the squad. Fortunately for Spurs they have no UEFA competitions to stretch their playing resources and only compete in domestic competitions. In Ancelotti's first season fourth place is secured plus a League Cup win. This creates an immediate wrinkle in time. In reality, Liverpool finished fourth and qualified for the Champions League, going on to win it in 2005. This victory is erased from the record books. It was this victory that convinced Steven Gerrard to stay at Liverpool and not sign for Chelsea and Abramovich's billions. Without this to anchor him to Liverpool he could be lured away to Roman's new club, Tottenham Hotspur. However, Real Madrid were always linked with Gerrard and the likelihood is that he would be drawn to Madrid rather than London and Spurs would miss out on Gerrard, just as Chelsea did.

In the summer of 2004 Chelsea made their big Mourinho signings, most significantly signing Didier Drogba, Petr Čech, Arjen Robben and Ricardo Carvalho. Tottenham would likely not move for these players due to having different connections (no Portuguese link) and a different formation.

Before Messi and Ronaldo dominated, the Ballon d'Or winners were often based in Serie A. The 2004 winner was an example of this. Having had phenomenal seasons with Milan under Ancelotti, recognition finally came the way of Andriy Shevchenko. Shevchenko was a favourite of Abramovich, signing him for Chelsea in 2006. The move did not work out. Signing him two years earlier and playing him under his former Milan manager increases the chances of Shevchenko being successful in the Premier League.

The midfield is further bolstered by again heading to Ajax. In this era Ajax possessed a raft of talent. As well as Zlatan they had Rafael van der Vaart and Wesley Sneijder. Van der Vaart would eventually sign for Spurs, but given that he and Ibrahimovic had a legendary bust-up this would no longer be an option. The move is instead to bring in Sneijder, another versatile attacking or central midfielder to offer further options in that area.

At Chelsea Wayne Bridge was eventually replaced by Ashley Cole. Though Sol Campbell went from Tottenham to Arsenal on a free, surely Ashley Cole would not reverse that journey? Instead Spurs look to France and Monaco who have a very attacking left-back of their own, Patrice Evra.

Adding these three players to the starting line-up gives Tottenham a team and a squad to deliver the Premier League title of 2004/05. Carlo Ancelotti would be well placed to win multiple Premier League titles and win the Champions League. His record for reaching finals of the competition is unparalleled. Tottenham could be the destination for almost any major transfer of the next decade.

Fabio Cannavaro could be drawn to Tottenham rather than Real Madrid after the 2006 World Cup by the presence of Ancelotti. When Dani Alves signs for Barcelona in 2008 it could be Spurs who sign him instead.

Huge signings such as these could have other counter points. Robbie Keane might have been a squad player rather than one of Spurs' greatest scorers of all time. Jermain Defoe likely never signs for the club. Gareth Bale moves from Southampton to a different Premier League side. Bale may never have become a global star. Does Harry Kane ever get the opportunity when Tottenham have the money to bring in any forward they choose? Abramovich's billions change careers.

Tottenham's trophy cabinet would have grown beyond all recognition. In 2018 a new state-of-the-art training ground was opened. Under Abramovich it is likely a new training ground opens far sooner. After many years of purchasing property around White Hart Lane the stadium was finally built and opened. The jewel in the Spurs crown, their state-of-the-art Tottenham Hotspur Stadium. Under Abramovich, this never happens. Plans to move away from Stamford Bridge seemed to be rolled out every season during Abramovich's time there, always promised but never delivered. It is highly likely to be the same situation at Tottenham. The club is far more successful on the pitch, but remains at White Hart Lane, rather than at the ultra-modern Tottenham Hotspur Stadium.

What of Chelsea?

Chelsea remain in debt and without a buyer, a situation that can't continue for too much longer. During this time there is another successful businessman on the lookout for a football club. A London-based entrepreneur purchased Newcastle United, but with Chelsea available surely they would be a more attractive option?

With Mike Ashley owning Chelsea their status could not look more different.

Chelsea's debts are cleared but investment in the team is minimal. There is nothing to draw José Mourinho to the club. Chelsea are no longer investing in the top tier. The first real managerial appointment of the Ashley era was Sam Allardyce, then a revolving door of managers, each lasting not much more than 12 months. The managers included Kevin Keegan, Alan Pardew, Joe Kinnear and Chris Hughton, until Alan Pardew was reappointed in 2010, lasting four years in the role. Steve McClaren held the role for around a year, then Rafael Benítez was at the club for three years. Steve Bruce was the final appointment of the Ashley era.

This list is not littered with exotic names. Or especially trophy laden names. Only Benítez had a track record of success, but his last trophy was the Copa Italia in 2014. He felt like a huge coup for Newcastle, as his appointment came hot on the heels of a spell at Real Madrid.

Chelsea had been consistently around the top four and would do well to stay there. Allardyce was considered a hot property when he was appointed at Newcastle. It is quite likely that Ashley would appoint him to very little fuss, though it would lead to a change of playing style. Chelsea would become far more direct, utilising crosses and powerful centre-forwards. Chelsea might finish in the top four a few times under Allardyce, possibly picking up a cup or two, which would be considered a success, but little more successful than the previous era. Ashley invested little in Newcastle's ground or facilities. Cobham would never have been the state-of-the-art facility and Stamford Bridge would be in urgent need of a facelift. Over time the quality of appointment and levels of investment would slowly drop, as would Chelsea's league position.

WHAT IF JIMMY GREAVES HAD STAYED FIT DURING THE 1966 WORLD CUP FINALS?

On 30 July 1966, Alf Ramsey watches his team walk out at Wembley for the World Cup Final against West Germany. He takes his place on the bench, a picture of studious calm. Sitting to the left of Ramsey is trainer Harold Shepherdson. Next to Shepherdson is a man in a smart navy suit. Almost every Englishman in the stadium thinks the man in the smart navy suit should be on the pitch. His name is Jimmy Greaves and he is one of the greatest goalscorers in the history of the game.

At the start of the 1966 World Cup, Greaves was an established name in the England line-up. Along with Banks, Moore and Bobby Charlton, he was a genuine world-class footballer. Yet he was more than that. He was talismanic. The one player every fan had faith in. The one player who could turn a game in the blink of an eye. Over 20 yards he was quicksilver, as fast with a football as without. Even so, the unique quality that made Greaves special was his goals. He scored all types of goals: tap-ins, thunderbolts, headers, left foot, right foot and goals that were unique to him. For every club, and at every England international level he played, from schoolboy to full cap, he scored on his debut. In the 1966 England team he was the undoubted star. For him not to be playing in the World Cup Final was astonishing, the equivalent of not playing Alan Shearer or Gary Lineker in a final at their peak, or leaving out Harry Kane from a 2022 World Cup Final team. When Greaves was injured in the final group game against France, and never returned, it's easy to surmise it was because the England manager wanted to keep a winning team. But for a perfectionist like Ramsey that would be an injustice to the level of professionalism and focus he brought to the England set-up.

Greaves made his debut for Chelsea in 1955, two years after Hungary had beaten England 6-3 at Wembley and had rewritten the long-established and widely accepted tactics of football. Up to that point attacking football in England focused on two wingers supplying crosses to a big centre-forward, like Tommy Lawton or Nat Lofthouse. Now came a different breed – forwards like Brian Clough and Greaves who were not big target men but who were quick, sharp and electric in the penalty box. The move from the old 'WM' formation with two inside-forwards playing behind a big centre-forward, to 4-4-2 saw attacking play evolve. Greaves was at the forefront of the evolution. Greaves scored goals wherever and however.

In the build-up to the 1966 World Cup, Ramsey very quickly settled on his first-choice defence. Banks in goal,

Cohen right-back, Wilson left-back, captain Bobby Moore at centre-half with Jack Charlton beside him. Nobby Stiles sat in front of them as a defensive midfielder. They played together in the vast majority of internationals during the 1965/66 season. At this point Ramsey clearly had no set thoughts on his front five. He played with orthodox wingers such as Payne, Connelly and Callaghan. He had a 'big man' up front in Peacock and then tried the lightning quick Bridges. Only Bobby Charlton and Greaves were guaranteed their place, it seemed. Then Greaves contracted hepatitis and missed three months at the start of the season. Some thought he had lost a yard of pace when he came back. Luckily his performance in the 5-1 Spurs' demolition of Manchester United at White Hart Lane is preserved for posterity. He set up the second goal with a peach of a pass that split United's defence. But it is the third goal which shows Greaves at his peerless best. He picked the ball up ten yards outside the United box with a defender tight to his back. He turned, lost his marker and set off towards goal. Defenders chased him, one lunged in, but the ball was stuck to his foot as he slalomed through and rounded keeper Stepney before passing the ball into the empty net. All this took six seconds. It was breath-taking. It was brilliant.

One of the key questions for Ramsey was who would play up front alongside Greaves. Roger Hunt had a stellar season, scoring 29 league goals as Liverpool became champions. Geoff Hurst too, had scored 23 league goals for

West Ham that year and many more in cup ties. It seemed to be down to those two. Ramsey's team has been dubbed the 'wingless wonders' and were widely acknowledged as playing 4-3-3. It is one of the great misconceptions. Ramsey settled on a 4-4-2 formation. Nobby Stiles and Bobby Charlton were fixtures in the centre, while the wide players were rotated until Ramsey found what he wanted.

England went on a tour of Europe before the World Cup started. Ramsey paired Hunt and Hurst in a 3-0 win against Finland. In the next game, a 6-1 win against Norway, it was Hunt and Greaves. Greaves scored four. Against Denmark it was Hurst and Greaves in a 2-0 victory. Finally, it was Hunt and Greaves in a 1-0 win against a tough Polish team. This was to be the last game before the World Cup started. Alan Ball and Martin Peters were the wide players. The only difference to the final team is that Greaves was in for Hurst. And even though Ramsey played Connelly, Payne and Callaghan in the group games, it looked like he had settled on his strongest team here. Knowing how meticulous Ramsey was, it is difficult to imagine he arrived at his best XI by accident. His rotation in the group games could have reflected how difficult he thought the fixtures would be and how inclusive he wanted to make the squad by giving as many players as possible a taste of the tournament.

What Ramsey created was a great team ethic. Even with world-class players in the side, it was the team that came first. Here we might find some clues behind the

World Cup Final line-up. Johnny Giles, one of the great midfielders of the 1960s for Manchester United and Leeds United, said, 'Jimmy always gave the impression that he didn't care that much, if it happened it happened. So he was totally relaxed and he'd score more goals.'

Was that something that went against the grain with Ramsey? Greaves was ice-cool in front of goal, never rushed or ruffled, he made scoring look easy. But did Ramsey trust him to run himself into the ground on behalf of his team?

Greaves' time in Italy with AC Milan had tested his temperament. Italian defenders were notoriously physical. Greaves himself thought it was the making of him as a player, even though he only appeared in 14 games for *I Rossoneri*.

'I always felt I went to Milan a boy and came back a man thanks to all the physical treatment I withstood from their defenders.'

But what if Greaves is not injured in the final group game against France?

He has not scored a World Cup goal yet, he has not set the tournament alight, Bobby Charlton's long-range effort against Mexico the standout moment for England so far. With holders Brazil failing to make it out of their group, Ramsey knows that Argentina could well be the hardest opponents England will face. He returns to his team that ended the European tour against Poland:

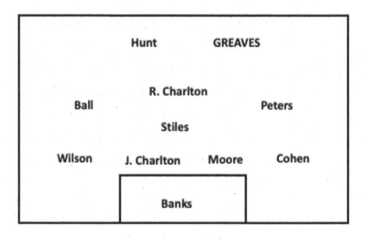

The Argentinians have done their homework. Right from the kick-off they set out to disrupt England's passing game, first through a series of 'physical' challenges and then through their captain Rattin, who is disputing every decision made by German referee Kreitlin. Stiles and Ball in particular are ready for the battle. Greaves struggles to get into the game as the Argentinian centre-backs Perfumo and Albrecht stop him with a series of niggling fouls. Then the pivotal moment of the game. Kreitlin has had enough of Rattin's constant disruption and questioning his decisions. Rattin is sent off. Chaos ensues. The game is held up for almost ten minutes as Rattin refuses to leave the field.

Eventually the game restarts. Argentina look more determined than ever. At half-time Ramsey calls for cool heads. With the extra man he knows England will never get a better chance. The second half sees Argentina dig in and they even look dangerous on the counter-attack.

England are watchful. Charlton is probing, but Hunt and Greaves can find little space. Just after the hour Alan Ball aims a cross to the far post looking for Hunt, but the ball clips the Argentinian full-back Marzolina and squirts towards the penalty spot. Greaves reacts quickest, steals half a yard in front of his marker and clips a shot just inside the post. The Argentinian keeper Antonio Roma never moves. England euphoria.

Argentina know their chance is ebbing away. They react to every England foul by rolling around. They look to get a man sent off to level up the sides. They attack with nothing to lose. Banks has to be at his best on more than one occasion. Bobby Moore is calmness personified. With less than ten minutes to go he sees Bobby Charlton in space. Charlton advances and draws the Argentinian cover before slipping the ball to Greaves just outside the box. One touch and Greaves sends a dipping shot into the far corner. The goal takes all the fight out of Argentina. England are in the semi-finals. 'Two-goal Greaves' is the hero of the press.

Ramsey retains the same line-up for the semi-final against Portugal, who have the tournament's leading scorer, Eusébio, in the side. Nobby Stiles is given a man-marking job to try and nullify the great forward. In complete contrast to the game against Argentina, under the floodlights at Wembley the two teams produce a game of quality football. The Portuguese have their totem-like centre-forward Torres as a focal point, with the ever dangerous Eusébio ready to pounce off his flicks and lay-offs. But Bobby Charlton is also in the mood and strides imperiously over the lush Wembley turf. After 15 minutes he plays a fine ball out to Peters in space and he crosses. Hunt makes a decoy run to the near post to leave Greaves in space and his instinctive diving header sends the England fans wild.

Their joy is short-lived. Minutes later, Stiles, who has tracked Eusébio's every stride, slips and leaves his man free. Eusébio plays a quick one-two with Torres and powers a shot past Banks. England concede their first goal of the tournament. The teams go in at half-time level.

Both sides come out for the second half full of attacking intent. There are chances at both ends. On the hour, Bobby Charlton tricks his marker on halfway and strides towards the Portugal penalty area. Greaves and Hunt take the central defenders away. Charlton dips his shoulder past Coluna, the Portuguese captain, and shoots. The ball hits the inside of the post and bounces across goal. Greaves is the first to react and from an almost impossible angle, he slides the ball home. England have the vital lead. There are some heart-stopping moments for the England fans as long-range efforts from Eusebio go close. The final whistle blows. As commentator Kenneth Wolstenholme says, 'We will never forget this night at Wembley.' Jimmy Greaves and his goals have taken England to the final.

On 30 July 1966, Alf Ramsey watches his team walk out at Wembley for the World Cup Final against West

Germany. He takes his place on the bench, a picture of studious calm. All the meticulous preparation, all the tactical planning, all the team talks are over. Ramsey, and the whole of England, expects his team to deliver. Much hope rests on the shoulders of Jimmy Greaves, but as the captains meet in the centre circle, he looks nonchalant, like he is about to play in a game on a sunlit beach. The emotion of the crowd, the deafening noise, sees a tense start to the game as the two teams struggle to settle.

Then an early goal. Uwe Seeler's innocuous cross is misjudged by the England defence and Haller moves smartly to shoot across Banks into the far corner. As often happens, the goal settles England as much as West Germany. They now attack with purpose and are not behind for long. A cross from Peters is half-cleared to Bobby Charlton. His shot is blocked. The ball breaks to Alan Ball. His shot is half-scuffed, there is a scramble and as the German goalkeeper Tilkowski comes to smother, Jimmy Greaves pokes the ball underneath him and into the net. He emerges from under a pile of red shirts, arm aloft. A hard-fought first half ends all-square.

England start to gain the upper hand in the second half. Roger Hunt goes close with a cross-shot, Greaves has a header scrambled away and Bobby Charlton shaves the bar. A corner taken by Ball is half-cleared. Jack Charlton of all people swivels and shoots. Tilkowski blocks but the ball loops back towards Peters, who smashes home. Delirium in the stands. The clock ticks down agonisingly slowly. Alan Ball seems to be everywhere. Nobby Stiles puts in tackle after tackle. Moore and Jack Charlton stand firm. But West Germany won't lie down. With just two minutes to go they are awarded a free kick and send everyone up. Jack Charlton heads away. Alan Ball is first to the ball as the West Germans try to reshape. Ball sees Greaves standing just inside the England half and chips the ball up to him.

Greaves has conserved some last gasps of energy. He sets off towards the West German goal, the ball glued to his foot. As he approaches the penalty area, Schnellinger has raced over from the left to challenge. Greaves drops a shoulder, wrong-foots Schnellinger, draws Tilkowski, takes the ball past him with his right foot and passes the ball into the empty net with his left. There are no people on the pitch, but the World Cup Final *is* all over, and England have won 3-1.

WHAT IF REAL MADRID GALACTICOS 1960 PLAYED REAL MADRID GALACTICOS 2002?

Forty-six million pounds. Seventy-six million euros. This is what Real Madrid spent in 2001 to land Zinedine Zidane from Juventus. A new world record transfer fee. Just 12 months earlier Madrid had set the world record, paying £36 million to land Luís Figo from their hated rivals Barcelona. The infamous Galactico era was well under way.

Each summer Real Madrid added a global superstar. Figo, Zidane, Ronaldo and Beckham were the most famous players in the world. All signed for the same club, to wear the famous all white and deliver the club's *raison d'etre*. The trophy that proclaimed them champions of Europe.

Sixteen champions from the European domestic leagues entered the inaugural competition in 1955 (notably the English champions, Chelsea, were forced to withdraw by the Football Association). The final took place in Paris, with French champions Reims facing Real Madrid. The Spaniards triumphed 4-3 with goals from Di

Stéfano, Rial (2) and Marquitos. Real Madrid's ownership of the competition began. Arguably it would never end.

Madrid won every tournament from 1955/56 through to 1959/60. Like the Galacticos 50 years later, Real would strengthen each season, becoming increasingly spectacular. Following the 1956 final France and Reims maestro Raymond Kopa was added to their ranks. Kopa went on to star at the 1958 World Cup. France lost in the semi-final to Brazil but they were prolific, Just Fontaine scoring an incredible 13 goals. Kopa supplied the ammunition and would win the Ballon d'Or in 1958. Kopa spent three seasons playmaking for Real Madrid before returning to Reims. In all his three seasons he ended up as a European Cup winner.

After beating Reims in 1956, Fiorentina would be defeated in 1957 courtesy of a two-goal win in the Santiago Bernabeu. Di Stéfano and Francisco Gento scored a goal each. Paco Gento played outside-left for Real Madrid for 18 years, appearing in 600 games and scoring over 180 goals. Gento won six European Cups with Real, including the first five competitions. Gento was famed for his searing pace and ability to run with the ball. He complemented the global stars, providing additional scoring and creating threat.

For the 1957/58 season Real added a central defensive star to their ranks. José Santamaria signed from Nacional of Uruguay. He would be the rock of the team for a decade, winning four European Cups. The first came against AC

Milan, Paco Gento netting the winner in extra time as Real Madrid won 3-2 in Brussels.

In 1958 Real Madrid added Ferenc Puskás to their ranks. They now had Puskás, Di Stéfano, Kopa and Gento in their line-up. The 1959 final was a rematch with Reims, a comfortable 2-0 victory. Notably this was Kopa's last game for Real. Equally notable is that Puskás missed the final due due to injury. He would not miss the next final, one of the most legendary games in the history of European club football.

Real sought to replace Kopa with another superstar, Brazilian playmaker Didi. Didi had starred at the 1958 World Cup as Brazil were victorious. However, it would not work out for him at Real Madrid. Allegedly there was jealousy between Didi and Di Stéfano, leading to a swift exit from the team for Didi. Not all was rosy for Real behind the scenes.

In the first European tie of 1959/60 against Luxembourg's Jeunesse Esch a seven-goal victory was recorded, Puskás scoring a hat-trick. In the quarter-final Real lost 3-2 in Nice but won 4-0 at home, with Puskás, Di Stéfano and Gento all on the scoresheet. The semi-final was a *Clásico* against Barcelona. In the first leg Di Stéfano netted twice with Puskás scoring the other. Two goals by Puskás and one by Gento meant that Real left the Nou Camp with another 3-1 win, to complete a comfortable 6-2 victory over the two legs.

The rivalry between Real Madrid and Barcelona has deep political roots. The position of Catalonia, dictatorship in Spain and the privileges given to Real Madrid have stoked the fires through the decades. Another element has been the competition for players. The Figo incident of the Galactico era caused riots but there were precedents.

Player ownership and registration can be a confused business in South America. In the early 1950 Millonarios of Colombia created their own super team of players from around the world. Di Stéfano signed for them from River Plate. Millonarios were not a FIFA-affiliated team at the time, so when Barcelona decided to try to sign Di Stéfano they went to the last team who held his registration, River Plate. Real Madrid then made a deal with Millonarios. Chaos ensued. FIFA eventually intervened, striking a deal that meant Di Stéfano would play alternating seasons for Real Madrid and Barcelona, beginning with Real Madrid. Barcelona refused to accept the deal and sold Real Madrid their rights to Di Stéfano. Barcelona missed out and Real Madrid profited with arguably their most influential player of all time.

Di Stéfano led Real through all five of those first European Cups. Positionally he was difficult to pin down, drifting around the pitch, acting as a deep playmaker one moment and then appearing as the centre-forward the next. Di Stéfano combined creation, dictation and prolific scoring all within one player. Slalom dribbling, long-range passing, mastery of playing with both feet. Di Stéfano dictated terms to his own team and the opposition.

In the 1960 final he ran the show in front of over 120,000 fans in Glasgow. Madrid faced West Germany's

Eintracht Frankfurt. Eintracht had scored 12 goals across the two legs of their semi-final with Glasgow Rangers and that goal threat remained in the final. Eintracht scored three goals through Richard Kress and two from Erwin Stein. Real Madrid scored seven, three for Di Stéfano and four for Ferenc Puskás. The final was a feast of attacking football and a fitting finale for five years of dominance.

When Puskás signed for Real Madrid he was many years past his career peak. He was already 31 years old, but still had the thunder in his left foot. Yet despite being past his best Puskás would help Real Madrid win three European Cups, but only played in the winning final once in 1960; he missed both 1959 and 1966 due to injury. In 1962 Real Madrid lost 5-3 to Benfica in the final with Puskás scoring a hat-trick for the losing team. He would play again in 1964 as Real Madrid lost 3-1 to Inter Milan. By the 1966 final the majority of the team who won those first five tournaments had gone, but Paco Gento remained. From the inaugural tournament until 1966 Real Madrid featured in eight out of 11 finals, winning six. The teams that followed would have much to live up to.

In Spain football clubs vote for the club president. This can lead to some outlandish promises being made by those seeking to win the presidency. Florentino Pérez promised Real Madrid fans that he would sign the world player of the year for Real Madrid from their hated rivals, Barcelona. Impossible. Improbable. Yet it happened. Legend has it that Pérez offered Figo millions to sign a pre-contract agreement that, should Pérez win, Figo would sign for Real. There seemed little to no chance of Pérez winning, so this was free money for Figo. Until Pérez did win and all hell broke loose.

As with the Di Stéfano affair, lawyers became embroiled in the dealings. Barcelona were the losers. Real the winners once again. Figo a traitor. A hate figure. When Real Madrid went to the Nou Camp the venom directed at Figo was immense. Missiles rained down on Figo. Lighters. Whisky bottles. A pig's head. But it was done; a world record fee secured the first of the Galacticos, the tricky, skilful wide play of Figo to feed the predatory instincts of Raúl and Fernando Morientes.

Real Madrid were already the reigning champions of Europe. A poor start to the 1999/2000 season saw them sack Welsh manager John Toshack and appoint Vicente del Bosque. They were only able to finish fifth in the league but beat Valencia 3-0 in the final thanks to goals from Morientes, Raúl and Steve McManaman. This was not enough. Real wanted a superteam, one to echo that golden era.

In La Liga it worked. They finished as champions in the 2000/01 season. The key signing was Claude Makélélé, protecting the defence and allowing a platform for others to attack. Raúl scored 31 times in all competitions to be top scorer. Guti was next with 18 and Luis Figo ended the season with 14 goals. The Champions League would have to wait as Bayern Munich defeated Real Madrid in the semi-final.

The 2001 summer only saw one signing made – the new world record signing of Zidane. Figo was a snaky, elusive, wide player. Zidane was an artist in the body of an ox. He had inspired France to World Cup glory in 1998, scoring two headers in the final against Brazil. He then played a huge role in France's 2000 European Championship success. Zidane's combination of strength, grace and poise meant that he could dictate a match against any opponent. Zidane was the best player in the world and now the Galacticos had two Ballon d'Or winners in their ranks.

Real Madrid lost ten La Liga games with two Ballon d'Or winners in the team. They started poorly in the league, climbed to the top of the table and then ended the season poorly. In the Champions League Real Madrid were imperious. The competition was split into two group stages followed by knockout rounds beginning with quarter-finals. In the first group Real won four, drew one and lost one, the defeat coming in the final group game when they had already qualified. In the second group Real won five and drew one, the draw coming in the final game having already qualified. The quarter-final was an opportunity for revenge against Bayern Munich. Real lost the first leg 2-1 in Munich but turned the tie round with a 2-0 win in the second leg. This set up a semi-final with Barcelona, paralleling the great Madrid originals. Zidane and McManaman scored to secure a 2-0 win at the Nou Camp. Raúl scored just before half-time in the second leg, making the score 3-0 on aggregate with a half of football remaining. The Barcelona equaliser hardly mattered and Madrid were into the final.

There, the Galacticos faced less glamorous but formidable opposition. Bayer Leverkusen chased a treble in 2001/02, finishing second in the Bundesliga, then losing the DFB Pokal to Hertha Berlin. In the Champions League they were the scourge of England, knocking out Liverpool and Manchester United in the quarter-final and semi-final. Bayer had multiple goal threats from Michael Ballack, Oliver Neuville, Ulf Kirsten and Dimitar Berbatov. The strong, classy Brazilian Lúcio marshalled the defensive line. Real's Hampden Park opponents would be no pushovers.

Raúl struck early for Real Madrid. Raúl was one of two home-grown Galacticos, a genuinely world-class forward, capable of creating and scoring in equal measure. At various times in his Real career Raúl was the centrepiece of the team or a key cog to allow exotic foreign signings to operate. Raúl played over 700 games and scored over 300 goals for Real Madrid in 16 seasons at the club. During the Galactico era he topped 20 goals in all competition four times, with one of those being a 30-goal season. A sharp finisher, his ability to produce a chipped or dinked finish was beyond compare. His opener in the final came from a run in behind the defence, his early one-touch finish catching the goalkeeper unaware and the ball trickling into the bottom corner.

Lúcio equalised. A free kick was delivered into the area and Lúcio planted a firm header past César. César had not started the season as first choice, that was Iker Casillas. Casillas made his Real Madrid debut as a teenager, won the Champions League while still a teenager and would win the World Cup and European Championship with Spain. Casillas' shot-stopping abilities made him a rare commodity, a goalkeeper who could be a match-winner. In the 68th minute César was injured and Casillas took his place on the field, making several critical stops towards the end of the game.

Bayer had restored parity but it would only last until half-time. The original Madrid legends had their iconic moment in Glasgow, and the Galacticos would too. Roberto Carlos, a Galactico from before the Galactico era, before the Pérez Big Bang, sprinted on to a pass down the left-hand side. In a typically attacking raid down the left, Carlos swung his powerful left leg at the ball, hoisting it high into the Leverkusen box. The ball dropped from the sky towards Zidane, his left leg cocked, ready to fire. The dropping ball was met by a sweet strike and sent spinning into the top corner of Leverkusen's net. Zidane had struck an audacious volley from just inside the penalty area with his weaker left foot. Most mortals would have struggled to control the ball, let alone shoot first time with their weak foot. Zidane was no mere mortal, however – he was a Galactico.

The Champions League was delivered. It was the only time the trophy would be won in the Galactico era.

In the summer of 2002 Real Madrid signed another Ballon d'Or winner – the original Ronaldo. Past his galloping best, with injured knees and struggling with weight issues, Ronaldo was still able to win the Golden Boot and fire Brazil to World Cup victory in 2002. Real bought him from Inter, their only signing for the season. Ronaldo scored 29 goals in all competitions but Real were beaten by Juventus in the Champions League semi-final. They did finish La Liga as champions, but for Real the Holy Grail is that Champions League trophy. Vicente del Bosque was sacked and replaced with Carlos Queiroz as yet another Galactico entered the picture.

David Beckham signed for Real Madrid from Manchester United. Not a Ballon d'Or winner but a global megastar on and off the pitch. This season was a disaster for the Galacticos, finishing fourth in La Liga and being beaten in the quarter-final of the Champions League. There could be only one solution – sign another Ballon d'Or winner. Michael Owen was added to the ranks, but he had a fight to get into the starting line-up with Raúl and Ronaldo commanding the starting positions. Real Madrid had three different managers during the 2004/05 season, finishing second in La Liga and being knocked out in the last 16 of the Champions League.

In the summer of 2005 Figo and Owen would leave the club. Summer 2006 saw the retirement of Zidane. The Galactico era was over, yielding huge amounts of glamour but only one Champions League. It is quite possible the

commitment to glamour was costly. To become Galacticos sacrifices were made. When Ronaldo signed, Fernando Morientes lost his place, a player beloved by the fans and players. At the end of the 2002/03 season Real Madrid released their captain Fernando Hierro, the heart of the club. Connectivity with the local fans was sacrificed to attract global fans.

Clearly the original era of Madrid megastars was more successful. Yet the early 2000s instalment of the Galacticos was iconic and has passed into legend.

If we cast our magic, getting the two teams on the pitch against each other, who would come out on top?

Eighty thousand people fill the blue-hued seats at the Santiago Bernabeu to watch Real Madrid's most successful team face off against Real Madrid's most famous team. The lush green pitch is set for a feast of football.

The Real Madrid originals won the right to wear the famous, pristine, all-white kit. The Galacticos wear their iconic all-black away strip. The black and white strips set against the luscious green pitch immediately provide a sense of occasion.

Original Real Madrid line-up in a 3-2-5 formation, their version of the W-M that was dominant in Europe for so long. In goal Juan Alonso, who started three of the five European Cup finals. On the right of the defence Marquitos, who was involved in all five. In the centre of the defence José Santamaría. To the left Rafael Lesmes, also involved in all five wins. At right-half is Miguel Muñoz, who captained Real in the first two wins and managed the team in 1960. Muñoz won nine league titles and two European Cups as manager of Real Madrid, eventually spending six years as the coach of Spain. The left-half is José María Zárraga, another five-timer. Outside-right is Kopa. Shoehorned into inside-right is Ferenc Puskás. Though more natural at inside-left, Puskás has been moved to make room for Héctor Rial, a five-time winner and scorer of important goals. Outside left is Paco Gento with Alfredo Di Stéfano is the centre-forward.

The Galacticos take the field in a 4-4-2 formation. Iker Casillas is in goal. Míchel Salgado is at right-back, with Fernando Hierro and Ivan Helguera the two central defenders. At left-back Roberto Carlos. Claude Makélélé is protecting the back four and allowing Zidane to drift around as a free central midfielder. David Beckham and Luís Figo occupy the right and left flanks respectively. Raúl and Ronaldo are the strikers.

Neither team is great defensively and this clash is sure to be a high-scoring affair. The Madrid Originals' three at the back could be in danger of being overloaded but their attacking force will undoubtedly cause the Galacticos problems. Di Stéfano's free role will challenge the Galactico midfielders. With Puskás at the inside-right position he would move into the centre-forward role, creating space for Kopa to drift inside from outside-right. Kopa prefers to influence games from central positions and the presence of Kopa and Di Stéfano gives the Madrid Originals twin playmakers. On the left side Gento would stay high and wide to occupy the Galacticos' right-back with Rial drifting inside. Rial and Puskás will both push on to the central defenders, asking many questions of the defence.

For the Galacticos their tactics are directed towards freeing the individuals. Defensively three players remain deep while the others are attacking, Makélélé forming the point of a triangle ahead of Helguera and Hierro. There is not a lot of pace in the central defensive pairing, but fortunately other than Gento there is not much pace in the Madrid Originals' front line either. Both Galactico full-backs like to attack. Roberto Carlos and Figo can combine wide on the left, with Figo drifting infield on to his right foot. On the right Salgado needs to overlap to create space for Beckham. This could be a major problem for the Galacticos on the break as there will be lots of space for the rapid Gento to attack. Centrally Zidane has freedom to roam, much as Di Stéfano does for the Originals. Raúl and Ronaldo will test the half-backs and defenders.

Neither team will look to press or counter-press as a strategy, though individuals may respond to triggers such as loose passes or touches. This lack of a pressing strategy from the Galacticos means that it is a level footing with the Originals, both teams looking to sit off when out of possession and not apply pressure until the ball has entered their defensive half of the pitch.

The Originals win the toss. With their first pass they give the ball to Di Stéfano. He puts his foot on top of the ball, surveys his kingdom, then fizzes a pass wide to Gento. The game is under way.

The Galacticos clip some early crosses into the box through Beckham on the right but Santamaría heads them away with ease. The Madrid Originals are in no hurry, stroking passes around, trying to get Di Stéfano on the ball. After a quarter of an hour Di Stéfano collects the ball near the halfway line. Kopa has moved infield, meaning Makélélé can't go to Di Stéfano. Di Stéfano is one versus one with Zidane. With a shake of the hips Di Stéfano glides past Zidane. Makélélé has to leave Kopa to engage Di Stéfano. A quick pass exploits this free space, finding Kopa. Kopa dribbles on to the Galacticos' central defenders and slips a pass to the now spare Puskás. A ripping left-foot strike puts the Originals 1-0 up.

The Galacticos respond immediately. Beckham switches the play from right to left, picking out the galloping Roberto Carlos. A pass infield finds Figo and the Galacticos have an overload on the left. Santamaría tries to cover the space but this leaves a gap for Zidane. Figo picks Zidane out and Zizou picks out a shot at goal. The ball rattles off the post but drops to Raúl, who calmly rolls the ball into the empty net.

Zidane gets on the ball once more. Under pressure from Zarraga and Lesmes, his trademark spin breaks away from both of them. Zidane shapes to shoot but instead slides a perfect pass to Ronaldo. Without breaking stride Ronaldo plants a powerful inside foot finish into the bottom-left corner. Galacticos lead 2-1.

Smelling blood, the Galacticos push forward. Beckham spots a Salgado overlap on the right but so too does Lesmes, who intercepts the pass. Gento has read the play and he is already sprinting into the space. Lesmes clips the ball into the gap and it is a race between him and the covering Makélélé and Helguera. They don't stand a chance and Gento is bearing down on Casillas. Gento lifts the finish high into the net for 2-2 at half-time.

Early in the second half Di Stéfano and Kopa combine to play around Makélélé. Di Stéfano strikes hard and low from outside the box but Casillas dives superbly to touch the ball around the post. The resulting corner is half-cleared to Puskás. He strikes powerfully but Casillas matches it again, pushing the ball over the bar.

It is the Madrid Originals' turn to get caught on the attack. Makélélé intercepts a pass and feeds Zidane. Zidane lets the ball run and fires a first-time pass ahead of Ronaldo. Though not as quick as he once was, he still has enough pace to catch up with the ball. Ronaldo faces Marquitos, shifts his weight to one side then back to the other, creating enough space to bend a shot into the corner. The Galacticos take the lead. With half an hour to go can they hold on?

Kopa drops into a deep position for the first time in the match. Puskás has pulled out to the right and Rial is against the central defenders. Di Stéfano has now found a pocket of space between Robert Carlos and Fernando Hierro. Kopa punches a pass into Di Stéfano. Hierro stands up against Di Stéfano, refusing to be drawn into a challenge. From nowhere a shot fizzes through the legs of Hierro and past an unsighted Casillas.

Now the Galactico defence is rocking. Rial slides a pass inside Salgado. Gento races on to the ball and cuts it back to the penalty spot, connecting just before the ball crosses the white line. Puskás runs on to the ball then thumps the first-time shot in off the bar. Ten minutes remain and the back and forth clash is 4-3 in favour of Original Madrid.

The Galacticos search for individual inspiration but it isn't enough. They are just that – a collection of individuals rather than a wholly coherent team. The inspiration was enough on occasion but it is why the Galactico era didn't deliver as many trophies as other eras. Defensively they relied on Makélélé to prevent the centre of the defence being bypassed and then on Casillas to bail them out after that. As they push for an equaliser Gento is in space again. Kopa picks him out with a simple pass. Gento sprints into the area, rolls the ball to the far post and Puskás rams in his hat-trick goal.

The Madrid Originals have beaten the Galacticos 5-3 in a work of art, to be hung on the walls of the museums of the world.

WHAT IF TECHNOLOGY TOOK OVER FROM THE REFEREE?

When the referee looked at his watch, saw that the ball had crossed the line and signalled that Edin Džeko of Manchester City had scored the opening goal in the game against Cardiff City, it seemed technology had finally arrived in football. It was 18 January 2014, and goal-line technology was now a part of the Premier League, the biggest and most watched football league in the world. There could be no going back.

For decades, football had resisted the growing call for technology. The principle being upheld, was that whether a match took place at Manchester United, or Ramsbottom United, it was played to the same laws of the game. Yet technology has been used in cricket since 2001 and in tennis since 2006. The desire to keep football 'simple', to have 'one game' played the same way at whatever standard, to have a single set of laws, held the game back from technology for far longer. It took a 'goal' in the World Cup of 2010 for football's authorities to finally bow to the pressure. England were playing Germany, and had pulled a goal back to be only 2-1 down. Frank Lampard's shot hit the underside of the bar. Replays suggested that the ball was at least a yard over the line. The referee waved play on. England's valiant fightback was halted. But the world was watching, and despite England eventually losing the game 4-1, the sense of frustration and injustice was palpable. Within two years, goal-line technology was sanctioned for use in the major leagues in Europe and in major international tournaments, such as the Champions League and the World Cup.

Four years later came the introduction of the Video Assistant Referee – VAR. The concept behind the move was to amend 'clear and obvious mistakes' missed by the on-pitch officials, such as offsides, handballs or whether a tackle should be a yellow card or a red. While goal-line technology, with its definitive binary conclusions, has been universally hailed as an improvement, VAR has caused enormous controversy. Not only does it seem too often to still rely on opinion or interpretation, but most match-going fans would say it takes too long to draw a conclusion. There are lines drawn, there are different angles, there are replays in real time and in super-slow motion. With goal-line technology the outcome is known within seconds. With VAR the outcome can take minutes, which in the cauldron of a Champions League semi-final can seem like forever. Critics say that VAR has taken the spontaneity out of the game, that it is difficult to celebrate a goal 'in the moment' as so many have been disallowed after VAR intervention. Advocates say that VAR gives referees the opportunity to overturn decisions that were wrong, and so the game is all the more credible.

What we know from decades of technology in all walks of life, is that sometimes advances are made through new concepts, and sometimes advances are made simply because the technology moves faster, results are achieved quicker, outcomes can be determined in milliseconds.

So what if all of this could be achieved in football? What if technology took over the game?

What would the future look like if it did?

Footballers no longer 'wear' technology, it is inbuilt. GPS trackers in a 'vest' under shirts are obsolete. Graphene and other two-dimensional materials enable technology to be woven into fabrics and support complex electronic data collection without any hindrance to the performance of the athlete. The concept of two dimensions is not an easy one, the material basically has no depth, so graphene is extremely lightweight yet incredibly strong and flexible. It is 200 times more resistant than steel and five times lighter than aluminium. But it is also an excellent conductor. Being an integral part of an athlete's kit means performance feedback is immediate and not only upgrades how analysts monitor players' heart rates and running distances, their speed and their acceleration, it also improves player welfare. Concussion can be detected in an instant so that players can be substituted immediately – there is no debate about whether they are fit enough to carry on. Analysts and coaches see who is struggling and can adjust their team accordingly.

Wearable technology is not confined to shirts. Every item of kit feeds back information. Graphene is built into socks and replaces shin pads. The speed and impact of a tackle is seen as clearly as that of a shot. Impact thresholds have been set, and this information is used to determine whether a player receives a red or yellow card. Wearable technology shows immediately which was the last player to touch the ball, whether the ball was touched before the player, and whether a hand was used.

To ensure that the technology operates to optimum effect, the players no longer wear a kit, they wear a football suit. It is a one-piece suit that includes boots, shin pads and head protection. It is made from a lightweight, flexible material that carries the most advanced technology. Footballers take to the field looking like speed skaters. The suit itself supports moving graphics on its surface with areas dedicated to high-definition screens. Players display sponsorships or advertisements any time the game stops.

Football fans love goal-line technology because it is conclusive and it is immediate. Wearable technology takes opinion out of the game. There are no grey areas, no debate about 'intention' or 'accidental', everything that happens on a football field is evaluated by technology so that all the decisions that affect the game are black or white. The proof is immediate, the stats and figures are infallible. In football, data is now king.

The effect of technological advances on football is autocatalytic so that change fuels change. Every line on the football pitch is monitored and is responsive. Whether the ball has gone over the touchline is now as absolute as the goal line. Whether a foul took place in the penalty area or not is also definitive. The interminable waiting for VAR to conclude has disappeared because the decision is instant. The concept of level in the offside law has gone. A player is a millimetre onside, or a millimetre off. The crowd knows immediately. The result is that goals are celebrated with certainty again.

The change that this fuels is one of the biggest football has ever seen. There are no assistant referees. All throw-ins, all offsides are adjudged by technology. The touchline changes colour to show which team has a throw-in. It's the same with the decision on goal kick or corner, the goal line changes colour to the team awarded possession. In fact, technology dictates all the important decisions in the game. Not just goals and offsides, but physical offences such as tackles and pushes. Whether a tackle is 'late' or not is no longer dependent on replays from every angle. Thresholds on the force of challenges are written into the laws of the game and free kicks are awarded when these are transgressed. Technology feeds back in an instant whether a hand has moved towards the ball or if the ball has struck the hand. The 23rd occupant of the pitch is no longer a referee, they are a facilitator, there to indicate restarts, to stop the game when players are injured, to allow substitutes to come on and off.

Technology takes over timekeeping. In 2022 the average time for the ball to be in play during a Premier League game was 54 minutes and 39 seconds. Critics of 'ball rolling' time won the argument. The game is now 60 minutes long but the clock stops when the ball is not in play. To aid player welfare, and as a trade-off with coaches, the game is split into four quarters. There is a two-minute break after 15 minutes and a two-minute break after 45 minutes with the 15-minute half-time interval retained after half an hour. Up to six substitutions are allowed, but none in the first 15 minutes unless there has been an injury. Time, like everything else in the game, is now definitive. There is no 'injury time', there is no 'added time', there is no 'man with the board' – every game ends after exactly one hour of play.

The new generation of fans want data. They devour data. Their opinions are based on it. Their enjoyment of the game has long been linked to it. Technology has fuelled change within football stadia. There are levels of hospitality still. But fans at live games have access to more data than those watching on TV. Their seats are those used by professional gamers and include a tablet device with a super-high-definition screen. Fans who pay the premium can see all the data the coaches see. They know the physical condition of every single player on the pitch. They have performance insights at their fingertips. They believe they have football intelligence because they can see it. Augmented reality gives them a feel for it that previous generations could not have imagined. Whenever a debate arises about who is having 'a good game', the data decides. Every major league in Europe, and all European competitions, insist on a minimum level of technology within the stadium. The cost of installation is prohibitive. Owners need to protect their levels of investment. Promotion to and relegation from to the top divisions is ended.

So, what if technology takes over football? There has to be a very strong possibility that after over 150 years the game divides. It is similar to the Webb Ellis moment when 'rugby' football became an alternative to 'association' football. What drives the division are the costs involved. There is not only the initial investment in technology to consider, there is the constant need to update stadia and the facilities required that will put the new version of football out of reach of all but the elite clubs. After all the recent debates it could be that it is technology that finally ushers in a 'super league' in one form or another. The difference already between the levels of technology in the Premier League and in League Two of the Football League are stark. It is not just the equipment, it is the level of staffing required to make the input from the technology meaningful. Many managers of lower-league sides have a choice that lies somewhere between an analyst or a goalkeeping coach. There would certainly have to be two versions of the laws of the game as it would be impossible for 'local' clubs to make the investment required. Most non-league clubs have financial debates about the quality of their coach travel, not the quality of their augmented reality.

Data has its impact on coaches and players, making both risk-averse. Players become inhibited, knowing that mistakes will be reflected in their stats. Pass completion, ball retention, shots on target become the bywords for excellence. Speed is still a much-sought-after quality. With up to six substitutions allowed, specific skills are used at specific times in the game. Players with the ability to complete take-ons rarely start as coaches try to outguess each other at the timing of their introduction. Formations change regularly through the four quarters of the games.

Football is no longer a single body. There is now 'The Traditional Game' and 'The Immersive Game'. 'The Traditional Game' is played by 'local' clubs; it has referees and assistants and is watched by fans who are mostly over 40. Some of its devotees believe it will become popular again in a way that vinyl became popular again in music. But to those under 40, it doesn't 'feel' like football anymore. There is no data to pore over. There are no statistics to analyse. There are no discussions about the expected goals created by the league's third-best number ten.

'The Immersive Game' exists in a 'metaverse' where fan engagement is everything. They watch the game from any one of the 22 players' points of view, they hear the coach in the dressing room before, during and after the game. The more they engage, the more rewards they get from their club. They may watch *El Clásico* in Baltimore or Beijing, but they are 'part of it' as never before. All-immersive, all-encompassing, all-conquering football that 'puts the fan first'.

The skills of old-time footballers such as Pelé, Maradona and Messi can still be found on YouTube. When it was a simple game. When it was a game played the same way by people the world over. When it was the Beautiful Game.